*regon South Coast*

# Canoe & Kayak Guide

### By Ron Wardman

## Westways Press
### Coos Bay, Oregon

## OREGON SOUTH COAST CANOE & KAYAK GUIDE
By Ron Wardman
Copyright © 2004 by Ron Wardman and Westways Press

Westways Press
440 Third Ct.
Coos Bay, OR 97420
(541) 269-5833
E-mail: *westways@harborside.com*
Webpage: *www.scod.com/guidebooks*

**When you travel roads, trails and waterways discussed in this book, you assume responsibility for your safety. Author and publisher assume no liability for accidents and incidents. Author and publisher cannot guarantee accuracy of information and cannot guarantee that tours are suitable for every paddler. Know and respect your skill level and that of others in your group. Please read important information in the Introduction.**

Library of Congress Cataloging-in-Publication Data:

Wardman, Ronald J.
Oregon South Coast Canoe and Kayak Guide

ISBN: 0-9658012-2-5

Outdoor Recreation – Canoe/Kayak
2.  Travel – Oregon
3.  Oregon Coast

# INTRODUCTION

Thank you for buying this book, and welcome to Oregon's beautiful south coast!

I've been having a lot of fun over the years exploring the inland waters of this region. From the lakes and streams of the Oregon Dunes and the Coast Range, to the estuaries and rivers that meet the Pacific Ocean, this is a paddler's wonderland, with opportunities in every season.

In my travels I've seen many vehicles with canoes and kayaks on their roof racks, but the folks in these vehicles always seem to be headed somewhere else. Figuring that perhaps people weren't aware of the many places to paddle around here, I decided to gather the basic information and make some photocopies to pass around. A few enthusiastic friends convinced me that the subject deserved a "real" guidebook, complete with maps and photos.

This book offers both saltwater and freshwater tours selected for their relatively easy paddling. For whitewater paddling information, check some of the sources listed at the back of the book. As for open-ocean kayaking, it's not recommended along the Oregon coast because of dangerous and constantly-changing ocean and weather conditions. Nor is this a comprehensive natural or historical guide of the area. Most paddlers are observant and appreciate their surroundings without a great deal of outside help.

## CAUTION!

Paddling is potentially a dangerous sport. Lives can be lost when paddlers don't follow safe paddling procedures. You must know and respect your skill level. Never try to overdo it.

Paddlers should be aware of weather, tides, and currents. All the waters of this region can be **cold**, with temperatures ranging between 45 and 60 degrees. **If you are immersed, hypothermia and death can quickly follow.**

While these trips are relatively easy, you must be realistic regarding your skill level. Try to paddle with a partner. Consider carrying a two way radio or cell phone.

Always carry proper emergency equipment and wear approved flotation devices. Flotation devices are mandatory in Oregon for children 12 years old and younger at all times in watercraft.

Always use caution when entering any water in an open boat or canoe. Don't enter surf, bays or other bodies of water during storms or heavy chop.

Some of these trips are in working waterways, so watch out for ships, tugboats, barges and log rafts. They all create a significant water disturbance that can easily swamp open watercraft such as canoes.

Paddle clear of boats involved in any sort of fishing activity or shellfish harvesting. Don't block boat ramps, access roads, launch points or shorelines used by anglers.

### ABOUT THE WEATHER

Generally speaking, the wind blows from the north in summer, and from the south in winter. Summer afternoons are almost always windy, so plan exposed trips for the morning, if possible. The sun's dazzling reflection on the water is another factor that can be minimized by paddling early on summer days.

Winter and spring storms are frequent but short-lived. It's not unusual to experience several days of calm, warm weather between storms; the southern Oregon coast is often the warmest place in the state in wintertime. Some of the best paddling can be enjoyed during these balmy interludes.

Storms also add a great deal of water to the area, influencing currents and water levels. You may be tempted into flooded areas, but use caution until you've learned the lay of the land (and water) or you may end up "beached" – *in mud*.

## ABOUT TIDES AND CURRENTS

Many of the paddles in this book take place within coastal estuaries, where a twice-daily tidal inundation pushes saltwater far up the inland waterways. Except in times of heavy rainfall, the tides always overwhelm the freshwater flow, so whether it's a flood tide (coming in) or ebb tide (going out), there's a very real push and pull. You can use this to your advantage, or be at its mercy.

Tides and currents are actually two different phenomena. Tides, as we all know, are influenced by the moon. Generally speaking, there are two high tides and two low every 25 hours, occurring about 50 minutes later each day. The terms high tide and low tide refer to the *horizontal* level of the water. At high tide, the water reaches its highest point, stops rising (called slack tide) and begins to drop.

Currents refer to the *vertical* motion of the water. Tides create tidal currents. Freshwater outflow from streams entering a bay or estuary also create currents. Hence at slack tide there may still be currents.

Estuaries with large rivers entering, such as the Umpqua River, have a strong outflow that sometimes hinders tidal inundation, so the flood current will be less swift. The ebb flow, however, combines outflow and outgoing tide to produce swift currents. In such cases there may not be true slack water.

Generally speaking, the current runs fastest in the middle of the channel, so if you want to take advantage of the current, that's where you should be. *If you find yourself fighting a current, move to the edges of the channel.*

The speed of the water increases as the shoreline narrows or objects constrict the flow. Watch for signs of increased flow by watching the movement against stationary objects or debris in the water.

Fighting against currents can be made worse by strong headwinds. Winds are generally stronger in the afternoon, so try to paddle in exposed places in the morning.

If you have your heart set on an estuary paddle and you've arrived at a time when the tides are not cooperating or it's too windy, *don't push it!* There are many excellent lake and river paddles within a few miles.

You should obtain a tidebook (available at local stores) and use the corrections for the places where you're paddling. Local newspapers print daily tide charts.

Many software programs that can provide tidal information are available for computers and PDAs. For my Palm PDA, I use *Tidetool*, a free Internet download at www.toolworks.com. Tide times are available at such sites as www.tides.com. For my PC, I use the program *Tides and Currents*.

I've noted the approximate corrections for high tide at many locations, but land observations should always be made prior to paddling. High tide is later as you go "upriver." The farthest reach of tidewater — the tidewater "head" – can be as far as 30 miles up an estuary, with high tide as much as three hours later than at the ocean.

The best advice is to paddle on an incoming tide. That said, you'll notice a couple of tours suggest using the last part of an incoming tide to take you up a tidal slough, and the outgoing for a return. On those trips, be sure you know where the channel is, since you could get caught on mudflats as the tide falls.

Ah yes, about the mudflats. In such places as Coos Bay, they consist of sticky ooze that's very difficult to wade through. Moreover, most tidal inlets and sloughs have steep embankments that become exposed as the tide goes out. It can be tricky to get in and out of small craft. This is particularly true in Coos Bay's South Slough and Catching Slough.

Don't get stranded!

## ABOUT WATERWAY HAZARDS

Coursing down freshwater streams and floating in with the twice-daily tides of coastal estuaries are partially submerged logs, tree limbs, lumber and other assorted junk, so always be on the lookout.

Pilings along sloughs and lakeshores are a remnant of the logging era. They're often rotted near the waterline, or may be partially submerged during high tide or high water. Keep alert for them, as they can capsize, pierce or otherwise damage watercraft. In general, they were placed in a straight line, equally spaced. When in doubt about missing or submerged pilings, paddle close to one you can see, and try to judge the distance to the next one.

## ABOUT WILDLIFE

You might see stately blue herons and snowy white egrets browsing the mudflats for a meal, or maybe even scare up some noisy crows or fierce-looking turkey vultures. You might spot playful river otters, or watch osprey build their distinctive nests built atop pilings and old snags. Multitudes of tiny shorebirds and colorful waterfowl abound.

Needless to say, keep a respectful distance from all of them. The western snowy plover, a threatened shorebird, nests in open sand around ocean estuaries. They're easily disturbed by humans, so several places are closed to public access from March 15 to September 15. Closed areas are well marked by signs, ropes, flagging and fences. At this point, no waterways are restricted, just the riverbanks and beaches. I've noted the areas that currently have seasonal closures, but new locations may be added and year-round closures are being considered.

## ABOUT LAUNCH SITES, DISTANCES AND TIMES

Launch site conditions are provided for each trip, as well as mileages and approximate time needed. You can follow recommended trips or tailor your own trek, whether doing an out-and-back trip or using a vehicle (or bicycle) shuttle.

Paddling times are based on fairly easy paddling of about

3 miles per hour, with time for observing points of interest. River and tidal currents can be used to increase speeds.

I used a GPS to determine the tour distances, and in many cases the waterway mileages vary from shoreline mileages, or, in the case of lake paddles, shoreline perimeters.

In the back of the book are US 101 mileages along the Oregon coast and highways over to Interstate 5 and other locales.

A note about the chapter maps: Because of their small size, they include only the most obvious features. They are generally close to scale and reasonably accurate. I have widened rivers in some instances for clarity.

Have a safe and enjoyable time exploring these many and varied waterways. Let's paddle!

# CONTENTS

# Contents

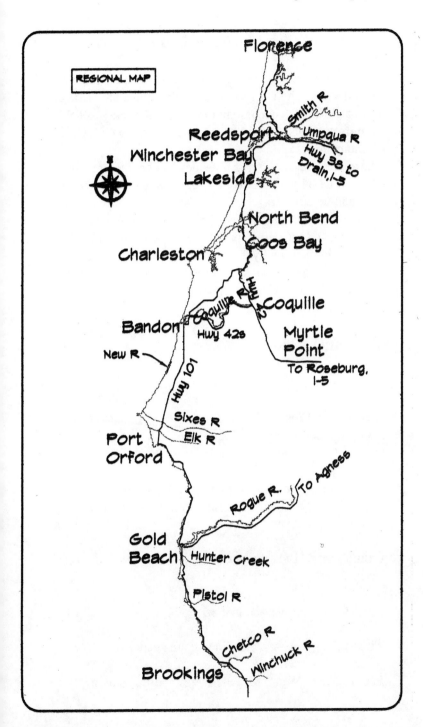

## Florence Area – Oregon Dunes

Florence is a jumping-off point for excursions to the lakes and streams of the Oregon Dunes. In this area are some of the coast's largest, deepest and most popular lakes, often set amidst forests that will have you thinking you're up in the mountains.

Some lie within the Oregon Dunes National Recreation Area, while others have sections of shoreline protected by state and county parks.

A few lakes drain into the Pacific Ocean, providing intriguing "lake to ocean" paddling, including one stream that's the only officially designated canoe trail in the region.

Large and small, popular or rarely visited, the lakes and streams of "Dunes Country" provide unique and beautiful paddling in every season.

## Woahink Lake

**Location:** 3 miles south of Florence.

**Directions:** From Florence, follow US 101 south about 3.3 miles and turn east on Canary Rd. In about 0.5 mile turn south into day-use area at edge of Woahink Lake.

**Facilities/Etc:** Improved restrooms, picnicking, swimming at day-use area. Honeyman State Park Campground is across US 101 from Canary Rd.

**Launch Site:** Boat ramp, dock, sandy beach at day-use area.

**Length:** 14.2 miles (perimeter).

**Time:** 2 to 6 hours, depending on area paddled.

**Precautions:** Watch for fallen trees and limbs along

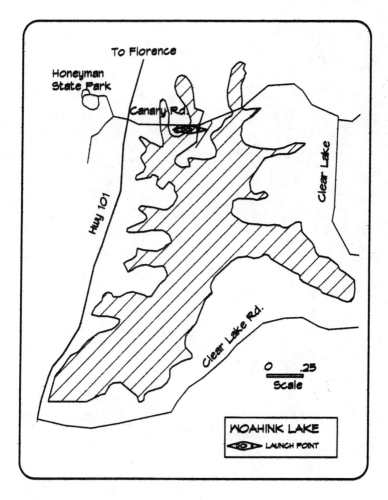

To Florence

Honeyman
State Park

Canary Rd

Hwy 101

Clear Lake

Clear Lake Rd.

0    .25
Scale

WOAHINK LAKE
◄◙► LAUNCH POINT

shoreline and in shallow water. Keep alert for fast-moving boats.

**Details:** Like many Dunes Country lakes, this one has a mix of shoreline ownership, with much of the land developed and some areas set aside as parks. The most interesting paddling is at the north end, with three inlets framed by tall firs and wild rhododendrons.

From the day-use area, paddle northeast and slip under the bridge to explore the easternmost inlet. To the west of the put-in, around the point, are the other two inlets. Not far

*Paddlers converge after circling a small island at the north end of Woahink Lake.*

offshore the day-use area is a small island to explore, while the lake's east side has a wide inlet that ends in wetlands.

## Cleawox Lake

**Location:** 3 miles south of Florence.

**Directions:** From Florence, follow US 101 south about 3.3 miles and turn west into Honeyman State Park, and follow access road to day-use area. Launch from boat ramp at "Y" intersection or turn left or right to other launch sites.

**Facilities/Etc:** Improved restrooms at day-use area. Rental kayaks, canoes and pedal boats available Memorial Day to Labor Day. Swimming area. Year-round camping.

**Launch Sites:** Boat ramp, beach at day-use area, and various easy shoreside locations.

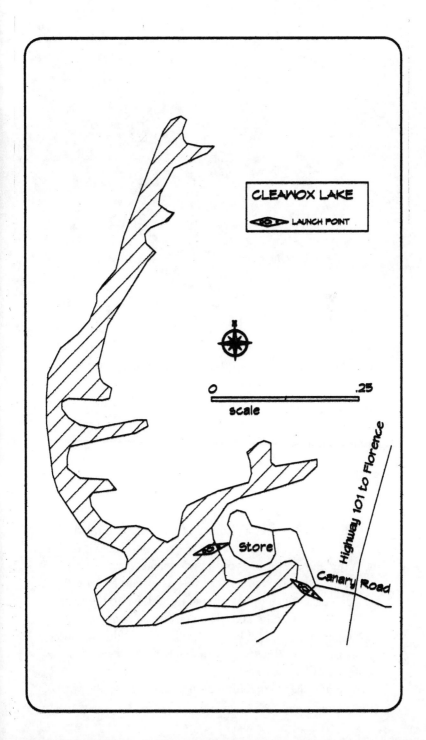

*Deep evergreen forest hugs the margins of Cleawox Lake's north arm. Find easy access to this jewel of the Oregon coast in Honeyman State Park.*

**Length:** 5.2 miles (perimeter)

**Time:** 2 hours.

**Precautions:** Watch for fallen trees and branches along shoreline and in the water.

**Details:** You only get a glimpse of the beauty of this lake from the roads in Honeyman State Park, but once you're in the water and exploring, you'll understand why this was one of the first areas to be set aside as a state park on the Oregon coast. Open dunes plunge right down to the water in the main part of the lake. The northwest channel is lined with magnificent old fir, hemlock and cedar. Wild rhododendrons tower over the waterways, while pink water lilies float placidly in the coves.

There are places to get out along the dunes on the west

side of the channel, but other parts of the shoreline are private property. A Girl Scout camp occupies some of the land, and there are custom homes along farther reaches.

## Siltcoos River Canoe Trail

**Location:** 6 miles south of Florence.

**Directions:** From Florence, go south on US 101 for 6 miles and turn east on Pacific Ave., following sign to Siltcoos Lake/Westlake Area. Follow Pacific Ave. to boat ramp at edge of lake.
*Alternate put-in at Lodgepole Picnic Area:* 1.3 miles south of Siltcoos Lake/Westlake Area exit on US 101, turn west at Siltcoos Recreation Area. Follow access road to Lodgepole Day-use Area.

**Facilities/Etc:** Vault toilets: Westlake Boat Ramp, Tyee Campground, Lodgepole Day-use Area, Waxmyrtle Campground. Overnight camping and facilities: USFS Tyee Campground and other private RV parks and rental cabins in Westlake/Dunes City; USFS Myrtlewood and Lagoon campgrounds in Siltcoos Recreation Area 1.3 miles south of Siltcoos Lake/Westlake exit on US 101. Boater/hiker camping: About 3 miles south of the boat ramp, on the lake's western shore, are a few hiker/boater campsites. (Hiker access is via Siltcoos Lake Trail, 1.3 miles south on US 101 of Siltcoos Lake/Westlake exit.)

**Launch Sites:** Boat ramp, dock, grassy shoreline at Siltcoos Lake Boat Ramp. Boat ramp at Tyee Campground. Dirt/sandy embankment at Lodgepole. Sandy shoreline at Waxmyrtle Campground.

**Length:** 6 miles roundtrip.

**Time:** 2+ hours.

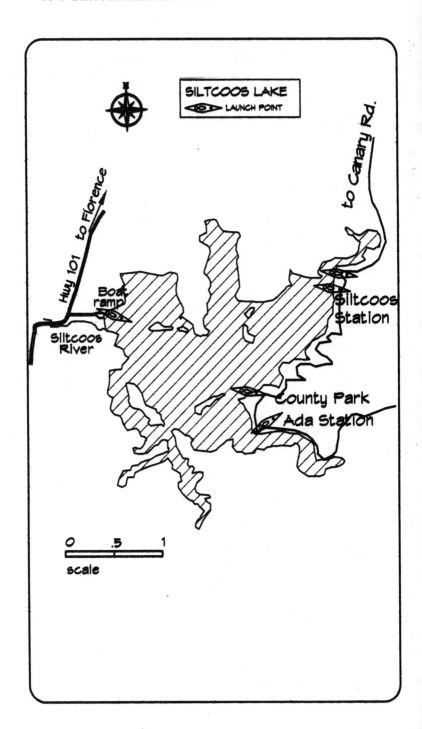

**Precautions:**  Summer afternoons can be very windy on Siltcoos Lake. Watch for branches and submerged logs in river. Fallen trees can block sections below the dam. Use extreme caution during high river flows as these trees – called "strainers" – can literally trap and drown you. Both sides of the river near the ocean are closed to public access March 15 to September 15 to protect nesting snowy plover. *Use caution at mouth of river and do not enter ocean.*

**Details:**  Oregon's largest coastal lake, Siltcoos Lake is a longtime destination for boaters, waterskiers, anglers and wildlife watchers. An often-overlooked "secret" is its 3-mile outlet to the sea, Siltcoos River, the region's only officially designated canoe trail. It slips peacefully from the lake through dense coastal forest and tall sand ridges, then loops into an estuary opening onto the ocean. There's a portage ramp around a small impound dam about halfway down the river.

From Westlake Boat Ramp, paddle south 0.5 mile past docks and marinas to the river entrance to the west. The river flows under a bridge and behind a few homes, and passes USFS Tyee Campground. The river slides under a US 101 bridge and leaves civilization behind for a while. The dam is about 1.5 miles along. Approach on the right (north) side. Depending on water level, you can paddle onto a concrete apron next to the dam, or you might have to get out and hoist up your vessel. A ramp/stairway completes the portage for vessel and paddler.

Downed trees and branches obstruct the river below the dam, but it eventually flows free again, passing USFS Lodgepole Day-use Area and Waxmyrtle Campground. Once into the estuary, there are sandy beaches on the northern shoreline. As noted, landfall along the channel as it nears the ocean and on the beaches is prohibited March 15 to September 15.

*A portage about halfway down Siltcoos River gets paddlers around a small dam. Pull your vessel across a concrete apron, then guide it down a ramp back into the river.*

# Siltcoos Lake

**Location:** 6 miles south of Florence.

**Directions:** *Westlake Boat Ramp in Dunes City/ Westlake*: From Florence, go south on US 101 for 6 miles and turn east on Pacific Ave., following sign to Siltcoos Lake/Westlake Area. Follow Pacific Ave. 0.3 mile to boat ramp at edge of lake. *North Beach*: From Florence, go south on US 101 for 5.8 miles and turn east on Clear Lake Rd. In 0.1 mile turn south on Darlings Lp. and follow it 0.3 mile to Darlings Resort. Launch fee may be required. *East Shore sites*: From Florence, follow US 101 south for 3.3 miles and turn east on Canary Rd. In 7.8 miles, you can turn west on Siltcoos Station Rd. and proceed 1.3 miles to Nightingale Resort. Or, stay on Canary Rd., which in another 2.2 miles becomes S. Canary Rd. and veers south. Continue 1 mile and at a "T" intersection just before a bridge over wetlands, go west on Lower Fiddle Crk. Rd. and follow it to Ada Resort. You can reach Douglas County Parks' Ada Boat Ramp by turning south on Ada Station Rd. 0.3 miles before Ada Resort, and going 0.8 mile.

**Facilities/Etc:** Vault toilets at Westlake Boat Ramp and Ada Boat Ramp. Floating vault toilet offshore Arrowhead Point (peninsula at north end of lake). Campgrounds, RV parks, motels and rental cabins in Westlake. Rental cabins and camping at Nightingale and Ada resorts. General store at Ada Resort. Boater/hiker campsites on west shore 1.3 miles south of Westlake Boat Ramp.

**Launch Sites:** Boat ramp, dock, grassy shoreline at Westlake Boat Ramp, Darlings, Nightingale and Ada resorts. Launch fees at the resorts. Boat ramp/easy embankment at Ada Boat Ramp.

**Length:** 27.8 miles (perimeter).

**Time:** 2-6 hours depending on area paddled.

**Precautions:** Strong wind most summer afternoons. Boat wakes. Speeding boats, personal watercraft, waterskiers, anglers, swimmers.

**Details:** At 3,100 acres, this is Oregon's largest coastal lake, so it offers a lot of potential paddling. It's relatively shallow, however, and often *very* windy on summer afternoons, so wind-whipped waves are a problem. Try to paddle in the morning.

A paddle south from Westlake Boat Ramp takes you by some hiker/boat campsites along the western shore, down into the three lower arms of the lake and back around Booth Island, for a roundtrip total of about 9 miles. From the boat ramp, paddle south, passing the marina and Siltcoos River entrance. Following the shoreline, you'll pass the first campsite landing in about 1 mile. Thick brush and trees come right down to the waterline for most of the way as you paddle past Booth Island toward Duck Bay, the first of four lower-lake inlets. The next is Harmony Bay, then Booth Arm, with reedy wetlands at their distant reaches. Retrace your route for a return, passing on the east side of Booth Island.

You can add a couple of miles to this trip by exploring Fiddle Creek Arm, the easternmost of the southern inlets. Paddle east from Booth Arm, slipping under a railroad bridge. The inlet becomes a channel through wetlands and ranches. Along the lakeshore just north of Fiddle Creek Arm is Ada Resort, a potential stop with picnic area and general store. From Ada Resort, head back toward Booth Island for a return to Westlake.

A paddle on the north end can take in the two northern inlets, with the easternmost one, Maple Creek Arm, offering some peaceful wetlands at the far end. There aren't many places to get out on shore, but you can stop and explore some of the small islands, or take a break at Nightingale Resort. Retrace your route for a total paddle of about 10 miles. You can add another 5 to 10 miles by paddling along the eastern shore, with potential stops at Ada Boat Ramp (go under the second railroad trestle) and Ada Resort. Just south of Ada Resort, paddle under a railroad bridge into Fiddle Creek Arm for even more exploration, then return to Westlake Boat Ramp by crossing the lake or retracing your route.

## Carter Lake

**Location:** 8 to 10 miles south of Florence along US 101.

**Directions:** From Florence, follow US 101 south 9.2 miles and turn west into USFS Carter Lake Day-use Area.

**Facilities/Etc:** None at Carter Lake Boat Ramp. USFS Taylor Dune Campground is 0.5 mile north of day-use area, with vault toilets at day-use trailhead and campground. Day use fee required.

**Launch Site:** Boat ramp, grassy shoreline. Sandy beach at USFS Taylor Dune Campground launch site.

**Length:** 2 miles (perimeter).

**Time:** 1 hour.

**Precautions:** Watch for submerged limbs and trees along shoreline. Strong north winds on most summer afternoons.

**Details:** This 30-acre lake might more appropriately be called a *loch*, since it lies in a long, narrow trough of the Oregon Dunes. Despite its proximity to US 101, it offers some peaceful paddling bracketed by forest and dune. The sandy beach adjacent to Taylor Dune Campground is a nice launch point or picnic stop.

# Tahkenitch Lake

**Location**: 6 miles north of Reedsport.

**Directions:**  From Reedsport, follow US 101 6 miles to USFS Tahkenitch Landing Campground and Day-use Area, where there's a boat ramp and dock. Tahkenitch Boat Ramp is 0.25 mile beyond. *Alternate launch sites on east side of lake*: From Reedsport, follow US 101 about 5 miles and turn north on Five Mile Rd. (Douglas County 49), a gravel road. A sandy beach launch site in 2.6 miles puts you into Mallard Arm. The road weaves up into hills and comes down to Five Mile Arm, with several put-ins beginning about 5 miles along. It's possible to paddle about 3 miles north from here, or enter main part of lake to west.

**Facilities/Etc:**  Vault toilets at both boat ramps. USFS Tahkenitch Landing Campground is adjacent to lake; USFS Tahkenitch Campground is 0.25 mile south. Unimproved campsites along Five Mile Rd.

**Launch Sites:**  Boat ramps, docks, sandy shoreline. Day-use fee at USFS boat ramps. *Five Mile Rd. launch sites*: sandy shoreline.

**Length**: 25 miles (perimeter), with additional mileage possible on Five Mile Creek.

**Time:**  Varying dependent on area paddled.

**Precautions:**  Watch for stumps and old pilings along shoreline.

**Details:**  With no development along shoreline or upland slopes, Tahkenitch Lake offers peaceful paddling, with many places to stop for a break or exploration. The arms and inlets and islands are home to birds and waterfowl; some open onto miles of waterways that can be paddled in

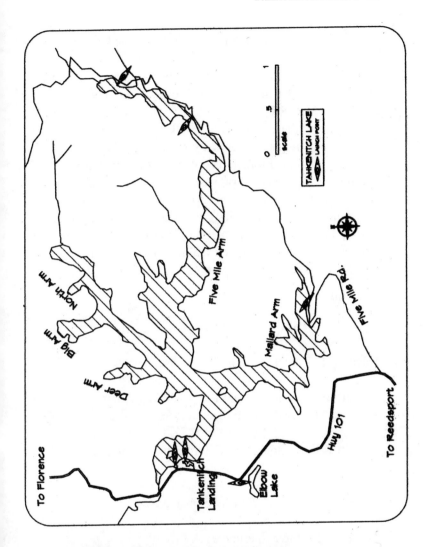

winter and spring. A railroad line runs through here, and there are trestles – some with swing-span bridges – crossing six inlets.

The lake can be arbitrarily split into a north and south end, divided by a line going east from the public boat launches along US 101.

*North section:* Distance up and back is about 10 miles, taking in a large wetland at the end of North Arm.

*South section:* Distance down and back is about 6

miles, with a smaller wetland area at the end of Mallard Arm.

Five Mile Arm to the east offers 10 to 20 miles of out and back paddling, depending on water levels. The launch points along Five Mile Rd., noted above, provide another way to access many miles of excellent paddling.

If you're feeling adventurous, you could paddle Tahkenitch Creek. From Tahkenitch Boat Ramp, follow US 101 north 0.3 mile and turn west into an access road to a small dam. Put in downstream from the dam. Fallen trees block the creek; at this writing three portages are required during the approximately 2.8 mile journey to the sea. But it's really cool, with the creek snaking through nearly vertical walls of sand in one of the least-visited sections of the Oregon Dunes.

# Elbow Lake

**Location:** 7 miles north of Reedsport.

**Directions:** From Reedsport, follow US 101 north 7 miles and turn west on dirt road to shoreside.

**Facilities/Etc:** None. USFS Tahkenitch Campground 0.7 miles north.

**Launch Site:** Reedy/brushy embankment.

**Length:** 1.4 miles (perimeter).

**Time:** 1 hour.

**Precautions:** Watch for submerged limbs and trees along entire shoreline.

**Details:** This little lake surrounded by steeply rising forested slopes is fun to paddle, although busy US 101 is in sight (and sound) most of the time. The southern arms are thick with lily pads that bloom with yellow and white flowers in summer. The lake bottom, like so many in Dune Country, is matted with the invasive aquatic plant *hydrilla verticillata*.

## Umpqua River

Largest river between San Francisco Bay and the mighty Columbia River, the Umpqua finds its source more than 200 miles inland, amidst the snow-capped peaks of the Cascade Range.

The Umpqua is famous for whitewater paddling opportunities farther upriver, but this book's coverage is limited to the downstream portions.

As it nears the sea, the Umpqua commingles with adjacent Smith River, and the two create a sprawling estuary, offering some very good paddling and exploring opportunities without traveling longer distances or doing shuttles.  And then there are the *islands* . . .

In addition to naturally occurring islands that remain or have reverted to their natural state, there are man-made islands. Like many coastal rivers, the Umpqua has been continually dredged to keep the waterway open for maritime traffic. In earlier days, the dredge spoils were dumped in specific areas of the estuary, eventually creating islands. These days, spoils are barged out to sea, and the islands have become *de-facto* wildlife sanctuaries. Unlike other settings, such as the small islands off the Oregon coast, river islands and dredge spoil islands are not (as yet) off limits. Here in the Umpqua estuary, as in Coos Bay, they offer opportunities for exploration.

The river bottom on approach to the islands is usually gradual, so landing is relatively easy. The footing is firm and sandy, as opposed to the quicksand-like mud found in other sloughs and estuaries.

As if this weren't enough to keep a paddler busy, there are also a couple of potential side-trips along the peaceful inlets of Smith River.

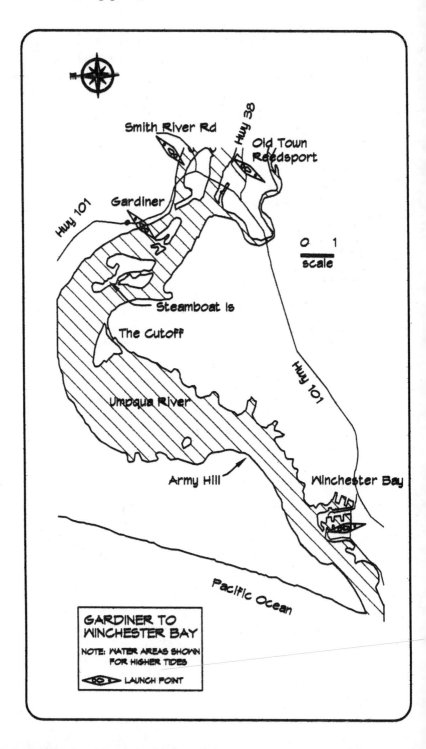

Expeditions can be launched from boat ramps in Winchester Bay, Reedsport, Gardiner and many upriver locations. You can really customize your paddling experience, depending on your energy and sense of adventure!

The twice-daily tides influence the currents on both rivers as far as 30 miles upstream, so be sure to consult tide tables. Tides and currents are strong! I suggest exploring these areas only at or near high tide. (High river flows in winter and early spring may overwhelm tidal currents farther upriver.) Do not attempt overly ambitious treks until you've familiarized yourself with the river, tides and currents.

Generally speaking, weather conditions (i.e., wind) and water conditions (i.e., wind-created chop) are rougher closer to the ocean, so the farther downriver you travel (Winchester Bay vicinity), the more careful you should be.

As noted, you can launch and take out from many locations. Here are a couple of suggested trips:

## Reedsport – River Islands – Gardiner

**Directions:** From intersection of US 101 and Highway 38 in Reedsport, go east on Highway 38. In 0.2 mile (just over railroad tracks), turn north on E. Railroad Ave. and go 5 blocks to boat ramp on the Umpqua River. 2 blocks east on Riverfront Way is Rainbow Plaza Boat Ramp.

**Facilities/Etc:** Improved restrooms at Rainbow Plaza Boat Ramp. None at Gardiner Landing Boat Ramp. Portable toilet at Bolon Island Boat Ramp. Reedsport waterfront area has restaurants and cafes, some open only in season. In the waterfront area is Umpqua Discovery Center, an excellent interpretive center and museum of history. Oregon Dunes National Recreation Area and Reedsport Chamber of Commerce share a visitor center at intersection of US 101 and Highway 38.

**Launch Sites**: Boat ramps, most with docks.

*A paddle down the Umpqua River from Old Town Reedsport's waterfront takes you past two vintage swing-span bridges. The first, in foreground, is a 1916-era railroad bridge that remains open except when needed by trains. In the background is the US 101 bridge over Umpqua River.*

**Length**: Loop trip as described about 10.3 miles. Additional exploration can add mileage and time.

**Time:** 3+ hours.

**Precautions:** Strong current. Paddle on incoming tide. Watch for submerged logs, debris and pilings.

**Details:** This trip takes you from the Reedsport waterfront downriver past Bolon Island and around the islands off the historic community of Gardiner, with a return via Smith River, where you'll pass (and pass through) even more small islands as you slip back into the Umpqua River. You can stop on most of the islands, as well as at Gardiner Landing.

From Riverfront Way boat ramps, follow the river west as it passes a swing-span railroad bridge and under the US 101 bridge (also a swing-span). Bolon Island is to the right.

You'll pass Schofield Creek's outlet on the left. Past Bolon Island the waters of adjacent Smith River merge into the Umpqua. There's a channel just before Cannery and Steamboat islands into which you can paddle up to Gardiner or return upstream via Smith River. Otherwise, continue downriver on the southern side of the islands. Once past the northern tip of Steamboat Island, swing northeast, with a potential stop at Gardiner Landing, then proceed upriver on the north side of the channel. Paddle under a railroad bridge, then under the US 101 bridge. You're technically in Smith River now. Bolon Island Boat Ramp is just past the US 101 bridge. Continue up the river past Bolon Island and choose a channel to paddle through to reconnect into the Umpqua River, crossing back to the waterfront boat ramps.

# Reedsport – Gardiner – Winchester Bay

**Directions:** *Reedsport launch sites*: see previous section. *Gardiner*: From Reedsport, follow US 101 north 2 miles to Gardiner. *Winchester Bay:* From Reedsport, follow US 101 south
4.3 miles and turn west on Salmon Harbor Rd. In 2 blocks turn north on Beach Blvd. and go 7 blocks to east harbor boat ramp. Or, follow Salmon Harbor Rd. and turn north on access road between the moorages, and follow it 0.5 north to west harbor boat ramp.

**Facilities/Etc:** Improved restrooms at Reedsport and Winchester Bay boat ramps. Camping, RV parks and other facilities in Winchester Bay.

**Launch Sites:** Boat ramps and docks; grassy embankments. Launch fee at Winchester Bay boat ramps, although with some scouting you will find adjacent free areas from which to launch or take out.

**Length:** Reedsport waterfront to Winchester Bay: 8.6 miles. Gardiner Landing to Winchester Bay: 6.2 miles.

**Time:** 2-4 hours depending on number of stops.

**Precautions:** Strong current. Be aware of tide times.
Wind and chop is common every summer afternoon and
may be a factor at any time of the day during every season.
Do not enter the river when it is "lumpy!" Watch for
submerged logs, trees and limbs in water. Watch for wake
from recreational boats, especially jetboats. Because of
strong currents and tidal influence, use extreme caution in
vicinity of Winchester Bay and do not attempt entry to
Pacific Ocean.

**Details:** One of the most intriguing and ambitious treks
takes off from the Reedsport waterfront and follows the
Umpqua River to Winchester Bay, near the river's outlet to
the Pacific Ocean. A shorter version takes off from
Gardiner Landing. This tour is best accomplished by relying
on the tides, and areas around Winchester Bay should be
explored in times of low wind (i.e., mornings). You can stop
at islands along the way, and make easy landings at many
places along the riverbanks. The river's flow, combined
with an outgoing tidal current, can be strong, so it's suggested you plan a one-way, downriver trip until you become
familiar with the indeed-mighty Umpqua. You might consider erring on the side of caution and launching your
downriver paddle during an incoming tide.
   *From Reedsport waterfront boat ramps:* Launch and
head west downriver along the waterfront, passing a swing-
span railroad bridge and slipping under the (also swing-
span) US 101 bridge. Bolon Island is to the right. You'll
pass Schofield Creek's outlet on the left. Beyond Bolon
Island to the right (northwest) is a channel to the Smith
River and Gardiner. Staying in the left (Umpqua River)
channel, paddle past Steamboat and Cannery islands. Once
past Steamboat, the river swings west briefly, then south.
   *From Gardiner Landing:* Paddle northwest and follow
the shore of Steamboat Island 1.1 miles into the main
channel. Depending on tide and river levels this area may

be shallow in places. Be careful to avoid hitting the bottom. Your path will turn west, then south as you pass the end of the island.

Continue along the south side of the river, paddling through the Cutoff, a channel that separates an offshore island on which you might spot cattle grazing (they migrate during low tides.) You can stick to the south side of the river and explore coves along the way to Winchester Bay. Or, once past the Cutoff, angle north across the river, where there are places to birdwatch or beach your boat and explore among piles of driftwood and sand dunes. The Cape Arago Audubon Society's *Birding the Southern Oregon Coast* notes that sanderling and western sandpiper are often abundant on the beach here.

As you paddle downriver, Army Hill looms on the west side. If you've crossed to the west side, re-cross just past Army Hill and hug the southern shore as you approach the harbor at Winchester Bay. By now, the current will be quite strong as the outgoing tide and river current combine. If you wait too long to cross, it will be a difficult paddle to enter the harbor because the current carries you past the entrance.

**Other Umpqua River tours:**

There are put-ins for many miles up the Umpqua River, but because of the current, most paddle trips require a vehicle shuttle. Generally speaking, the river is clear of obstructions and rapids from Scottsburg on down (about 16 miles.) Just above Scottsburg is Sawyer's Rapids, a class III rapids. Beyond that the river returns to a relatively placid state for about 3 miles. Farther upriver the conditions vary with the season. Winter and early spring bring robust flow through a succession of rapids and flats. As the season progresses and water levels drop these turn into easier paddles, with many shallow areas, quiet eddies and fun chutes through the smoothed-over rocks. Short portages may be necessary.

Even in summer, however, the Umpqua is a powerful river with a strong current, so use caution!

Highway 38 follows the river for many miles, and a handful of public boat ramps offer access.

Upriver access points along Highway 38 from US 101 intersection in Reedsport:

*Dean Creek Elk Viewing Area:* 3 miles. Informal put-ins along grassy/reedy banks offer access to an inner channel of Umpqua River. Improved restroom in viewing area.
*Umpqua Wayside (Brandy Bar):* 8.7 miles. Boat ramp. Vault toilet.
*Scottsburg Park:* 15.2 miles. Boat ramp, seasonal docks, improved restroom.
*Scott Creek:* 25.2 miles. Boat ramp, vault toilet.
*Bunch Bar:* 30 miles. Boat ramp, vault toilet.

## Schofield Creek

**Location:** Reedsport. (Tributary/slough of Umpqua River.)

**Directions:** *Umpqua River put-ins:* From US 101 and Highway 38 intersection in Reedsport, go east on Highway 38. In 0.2 mile turn north on East Railroad Ave. Follow it 5 blocks to boat ramp at Umpqua River. Rainbow Plaza Boat Ramp is two blocks north on Riverfront Way

*Coho RV Park put-in:* From US 101 and Highway 38 intersection in Reedsport, go south on US 101 7 blocks and turn east into Coho RV Park. Ask permission at office to use boat ramp at north end of RV park.

*Schofield Rd. put-in:* From US 101 and Highway 38 intersection in Reedsport, go east on Highway 38 for about 2 miles and turn south on Schofield Rd. (Schofield Disposal Site.) Oar Creek is about 2 miles, with a potential put-in in a reedy but stable spot at the south end of the bridge. Thorton Oar Ln. is 1 mile beyond. Turn west

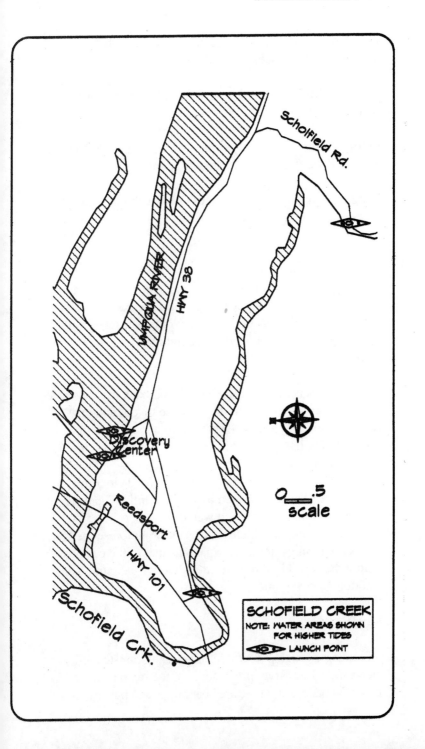

and follow gravel road to potential put-in on reedy but
stable ground just before the bridge.

**Facilities/Etc:** Improved restrooms at Rainbow Plaza
Boat Ramp.

**Launch Sites:** Boat ramps and docks at Umpqua River
put-ins. Reedy/brush embankments at upslough sites.

**Length:** Umpqua River put-in to Oar Creek take-out 5.6
miles one way.

**Time:** 2+ hours.

**Precautions:** Consult tide tables and start well before high
tide. Current runs strong with higher tide levels. On this
trip, be especially watchful for rotten pilings just below the
surface. As always, be alert for submerged logs, trees and
limbs.

**Details:** This is a relatively easy out and back trip, and also
fun if you do a vehicle shuttle. Start the trek at Umpqua
River put-ins, and follow the river west about 0.7 mile,
turning south into Schofield Creek. The creek flows through
Reedsport, passing schools, homes, businesses and RV
parks. It slips under a US 101 bridge. Beyond city limits
beautiful wetlands are ringed by forested hills. The watery
expanse is home to birds and waterfowl.

If you're doing a vehicle shuttle and want to use the Oar
Creek take-out, watch for a small channel to the east just
before the second railroad trestle. Otherwise continue to
Thorton Oar take-out.

# Smith River

Flowing through peaceful farmlands and forested hill-
sides, the Smith River offers some of the region's most
beautiful paddling. There are boat ramps and put-ins all

along the way. The Smith meets the Umpqua River near Reedsport, forming a diverse estuary discussed in the previous section. Tidal influence reaches about 20 miles up Smith River, so you can use the tides to your advantage on both out-and-back treks or one-way paddles.

The head of tidewater is also about the limit of practical paddling. Paddle trips vary in length and time depending upon your launch point, logistics and ambition. The river also offers good angling during the various fish runs, so be prepared for boats and fisherman.

Hudson and Otter sloughs, about 3 miles upriver from Reedsport, are potential detours, or tours in themselves.

Use the map and information on distances and tidal corrections at the end of this section to customize a Smith River trip, or combine it with a paddle in the Umpqua River, discussed in the previous section.

**Location:** Just north of Reedsport.

**Directions:** From Reedsport, go north on US 101, cross-ing Umpqua River Bridge. About 1 mile north of Reedsport, turn east on Smith River Rd. In 200 feet turn north to Bolon Island Boat Ramp. Continue upriver to other launch sites.

**Launch Sites** (All mileages from US 101/Smith River Rd. junction):
*Bolon Island Boat Ramp:* .01 mile. Boat ramp and adja-cent bushy embankment.
*South Side Rd:* 3.2 miles. Turn south and cross the bridge. Immediately past bridge is parking area and sign for Dawson and Stowe Marsh, a wetland restoration area. A short, adjacent track leads to river's edge with grassy/reedy put-in. See next trip for more details.
*Hudson Slough:* 3.3 miles. Emergency use only. Brushy embankment.
*Sandy Beach put-in*: 5 miles. Sandy, flat shoreline.
*Smith River Marina/RV Park:* 7.7 miles. Boat ramp,

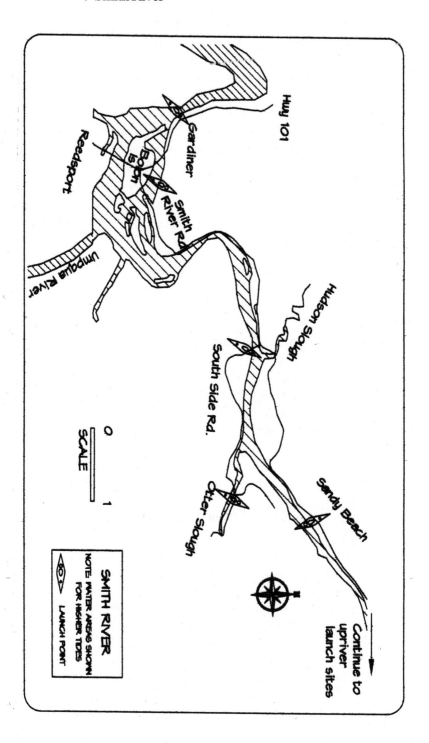

docks, embankment.

*USFS Noel Ranch Boat Ramp:* 8.4 miles. Boat ramp, grassy shoreline.

*Riverside County Park Boat Ramp:* 11.1 miles. Boat ramp, grassy shoreline.

*Smith River Timber Access Rd. System sign/put-in:* 13.1 miles. Unofficial put-in used by drift boat anglers. Gently sloped dirt/grassy embankment.

*Private bridge put-in:* 17.5 miles. Just before bridge is road down to river used by drift boat anglers.

*Spencer Creek (head of tidewater):* 19.3 miles.

**Facilities/Etc:** Portable toilet at Bolon Island Boat Ramp; vault toilets at Riverside County Park and USFS Noel Ranch Boat Ramp. Community of Smith River (14.5 miles) has general store, café, tavern.

**Time:** 2+ hours depending on length of trip and tidal current.

**Precautions:** Be aware of tide times and plan trips accordingly. Tides and currents can be strong! Watch for floating or submerged logs. Watch for pilings along river edges. Your potential launch points or take-outs may be shared with shoreline and/or driftboat anglers, so be respectful and do not block access roads.

**Details:** As noted, the Smith River offers out-and-back options or shuttle-assisted paddles. Wherever you launch, consider using the final hours of an incoming tide for a trip upriver, then let the current and ebbing tide carry you back. High tide at Sandy Beach put-in is about 1 hour 20 minutes later than high tide in Reedsport; about 2 hours later at head of tidewater.

*Paddlers return to the main Smith River channel after a trek up Otter Slough, one of two potential side trips.*

## Smith River – Otter and Hudson Sloughs

**Location:** Just north of Reedsport.

**Directions:** From Reedsport, follow US 101 north, crossing Umpqua River Bridge. About 1 mile north of Reedsport, turn east on Smith River Rd. In about 3 miles, turn south on South Side Rd., crossing a bridge. Immediately past the bridge is parking area and sign for Dawson and Stowe Marsh. A short trail leads to river's edge.

**Facilities/Etc:** Wetland/wildlife viewing area at Stowe and Dawson Marsh.

**Launch Sites:** Sandy/brushy/reedy embankments.

**Length (from South Side Bridge put-in):** Hudson Slough: 4 miles roundtrip. Otter Slough: 3.9 miles roundtrip.

**Time:** 1 hour for each.

**Precautions:** Be aware of tide times and plan trips accordingly. Tides and currents can be strong! Watch for floating or submerged logs. Watch for pilings along river edges. Your potential launch points or take-outs may be shared with shoreline anglers or driftboat fishermen, so be respectful and do not block access roads.

**Details:** These two Smith River sloughs offer beautiful paddling, and can be combined with other trips, done together, or paddled individually. Launch about 1 hour before high tide for Reedsport. Birdlife is abundant; you'll notice many wooden birdhouses set on pilings throughout the marshlands.

*Hudson Slough:* From launch site, paddle across Smith River and head upriver about 0.2 mile, turning west into the slough, which twists back into surrounding hills. Most of the shoreline is private property, so there aren't many places to get out.

*Otter Slough:* From launch site, paddle about 1 mile up Smith River and turn south into the slough. In 0.6 mile is a bridge with adjacent potential landing/take-out site. The slough swings south and encounters another bridge in 0.6 mile. It's too low to paddle under, but you could portage it and follow the narrowing, but still tidally influenced slough another half-mile or so, depending on water levels.

# Loon Lake

**Location:** 20 miles east of Reedsport.

**Directions:** From Reedsport, follow Highway 38 13 miles and turn south on Mill Creek Rd. Follow it 7 miles and enter the BLM Loon Lake Campground (Open May 31 - Nov. 1). In off-season, continue 1.2 miles to BLM East Shore site, or 2.5 miles to Fish Haven Resort.

**Facilities/Etc:** Improved restrooms, RV sites, campground, picnic tables, swimming beach at BLM Loon Lake site. Vault toilets, camping at BLM East Shore site. Improved restrooms, RV sites, camping at Fish Haven Resort.

**Launch Sites:** Boat ramp, docks, sandy beach at BLM Loon Lake site. Grassy shoreline at East Shore site. Boat ramp, docks at Fish Haven Resort. Day-use fees at BLM sites; launch fee at Fish Haven Resort (inquire at Loon Lake Lodge 0.5 north of Fish Haven Resort.)

**Length:** 4.2 miles (perimeter).

**Time:** 2+ hours.

**Precautions:** Watch for floating logs and branches.

**Details:** Set amidst Coast Range forests and well protected from summer fog and wind, Loon Lake is popular with waterskiers, boaters and personal watercraft enthusiasts, so it's an early-morning or evening paddle during that time of year. In the off-season, it's peaceful all day long, and you may even encounter (or hear) the lake's namesake bird.

# Lake Marie

**Location:** Within Umpqua Lighthouse State Park, near Winchester Bay.

**Directions:** From north end of McCullough Bridge, follow US 101 north 16 miles and turn west on Umpqua Lighthouse Rd. Follow signs to lighthouse. Lake Marie is 0.25 mile west of state park campground.

**Facilities/Etc:** Restrooms, picnic area, swimming beach, lake loop trail. Adjacent Umpqua Lighthouse State Park Campground has rental yurts. Nearby lighthouse is open for tours; museum open seasonally.

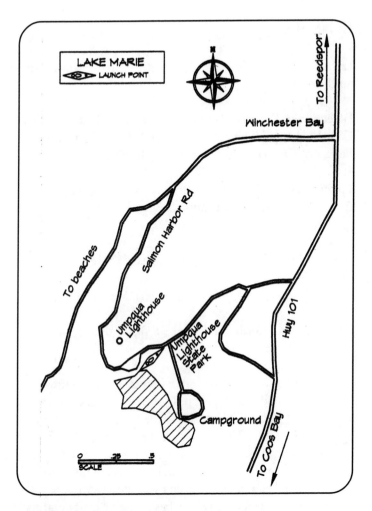

**Launch Site:** Sandy beach.

**Length:** 1 mile (perimeter).

**Time:** 1 hour.

**Precautions:** Stumps and limbs.

**Details:** Pretty little lake in forested setting offers easy paddling for families and first-time paddlers.

# Eel Lake

**Location:** Adjacent to William Tugman State Park, 1 mile north of Lakeside.

**Directions:** From north end of McCullough Bridge, follow US 101 11.8 miles and turn east into William Tugman State Park. Follow road to parking area at lake's edge.

**Facilities/Etc:** Improved restrooms, showers, picnic area, fishing dock, hiker/biker trails, Oregon State Parks campground.

**Launch Site:** Boat ramp, sandy/ grassy shoreline.

**Length/Time:** 11.5 miles (perimeter). See "Details."

**Precautions:** North wind can be a factor during summer afternoons.

**Details:** With a 5-mph motorboat speed limit and most of its shoreline and forested slopes protected from development, this 355-acre, horseshoe-shaped lake is a great place for a quiet paddle. There's easy, excellent access from Tugman State Park on the west side, just off US 101. The lake's many coves and surrounding woods are home to osprey, ducks and other birds and waterfowl. Anglers pursue stocked trout as well as bass. The lake's two arms conveniently "split" in the area directly in front of the boat launch.

**West Arm**: At the upper end is a nice wetland that can be paddled depending upon lake level; of historic interest are the remains of old logging trestles.

**Length:** 2.8 miles round trip.

**Time:** 1+ hour.

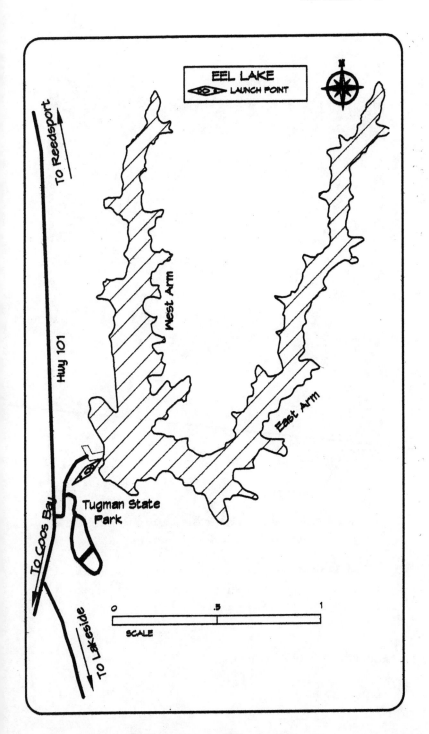

*A canoeist takes to the waters of Eel Lake.*

**East Arm**:  Many small coves offer intriguing detours, and some have places to pull into and get out. A hiking/ mountain bike trail follows part of the south shore, with overlooks and informal landings.

**Length:**  5.2 miles round trip.

**Time:**  2+ hours.

# Ten Mile Lakes

**Location:** About 12 miles north of Coos Bay/North Bend area.

**Directions:** From north end of McCullough Bridge, follow US 101 north 10.3 miles and turn east on Airport Way, following signs to Lakeside. In 0.6 mile bear south on N. 8th St and in 3 blocks turn east on Park Avenue, following it 3 blocks to Lakeside County Park.

**Facilities/Etc:** Improved restrooms, picnic area, fishing dock. Two floating portable toilets, one in North Lake and the other in South Lake. Motels, RV parks and campgrounds nearby.

**Launch Site:** Boat ramp, docks, sandy beach at Ten Mile Lakes County Park.
*Alternate Launch Sites:* Boat ramp at south end of 8th (or "Main") St., just past Hilltop Drive. This puts you into Ten Mile Creek downstream from the lake. There's another boat ramp two blocks west of 8th St. along Park Ave.

**Length:** North Ten Mile Lake: 19.3 miles (perimeter).
South Ten Mile Lake: 23 miles (perimeter).

**Time:** Varying depending on amount paddled.

**Precautions:** Boat wakes. Speeding boats, personal watercraft, waterskiers, anglers, swimmers and racing sailboats.

**Details:** Ten Mile Lakes, as the name might imply, are actually two lakes connected by a channel, offering an impressive surface area of 2,727 acres (that's more than 42 miles of shoreline). Said to be the second-most popular recreational lake in Oregon, it's certainly the busiest and most developed of the many freshwater lakes between

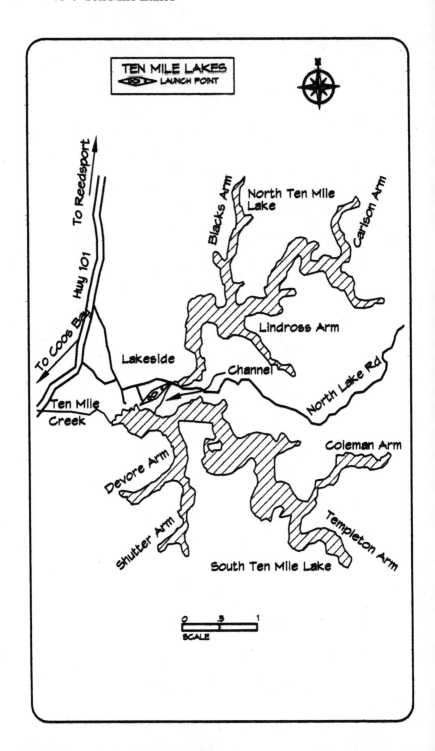

*Kayaks await an outing on Ten Mile Lakes.*

Coos Bay and Florence. The lakes are popular with anglers, waterskiers, personal watercraft operators and pleasure boaters. On summer weekends, expect a lot of

boat wake and high-speed traffic; there's much less activity on weekdays and in the off-season.

Much of the shoreline is private property, so landing is pretty much limited to the public boat ramp, a couple of private marinas, and some spots at the distant arms of each lake.

At the far end of North Lake are places to land under the train trestle in Black's Arm. Other North Lake picnic spots are at the ends of Carlson Arm and Big Arm.

At the eastern reaches of South Lake, there's a sandy beach at the end of Coleman Arm, while nearby Templeton Arm can sometimes offer places to land where Johnson Creek flows into the lake.

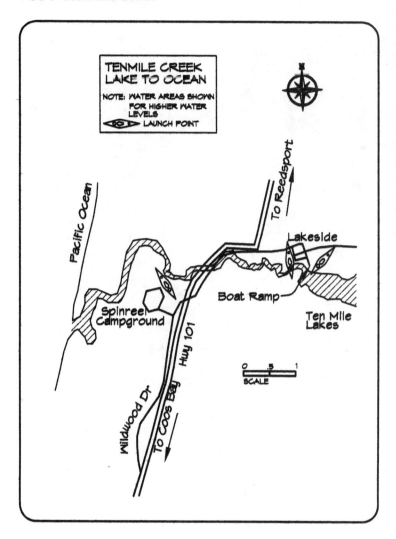

## Ten Mile Creek

**Location/Directions/Facilities/Launch Sites**: See
previous tour.

*Alternate launch site:* USFS Spinreel Campground. From
north end of McCullough Bridge, follow US 101 north 9
miles and turn west on Spinreel Rd., following it to campground. Boat ramp is adjacent to parking area beyond
campground. Day-use fee.

*Ten Mile Creek passes through a wide mix of terrain and scenery. It flows from Ten Mile Lakes through peaceful forests and tall, jungly brush and grasses. . .*

**Length:**  Lakeside Boat Ramp to Pacific Ocean:  6 miles. Spinreel Campground to Pacific Ocean: 3 miles

**Time:**  3+ hours (entire tour round trip).

**Precautions:** Ten Mile Creek has a deceptively strong current. Downed trees and brush may completely block channel at times, which during high flows can create potentially deadly strainers. Watch for submerged trees, limbs, and roots. Use caution around the railroad bridge as there are many cut-off pilings. North wind can be strong in summertime from Spinreel Campground to the Pacific Ocean. Use caution around river mouth and ocean. The creek level can raise 2 to 4+ feet during times of high water.

**Details:** This paddle offers quite a challenge if you do the whole trek out and back from Ten Mile Lakes, but you can cut the mileage in half with a put-in at USFS Spinreel

*. . . to the shifting sands and open expanses of the Oregon Dunes. Downriver from Spinreel Campground is this view of a "tree island," a remnant of forest surrounded by dunes.*

Campground, farther down the creek. The whole trip offers one of the region's most interesting, mainly because the terrain changes so much. You start in the forests around Ten Mile Lakes and slowly make a transition to wind-sculpted sand dunes, eventually reaching the sea.

Starting from the beach in Ten Mile County Park in Lakeside, paddle west 0.3 mile to the creek's outlet. The creek passes between marinas and shoreside homes, and goes by two other boat ramps. It weaves through reeds, willows and trees, then passes under the railroad and US 101 bridges, respectively. It meanders past more homes, and 3 miles downstream from the lake, passes Spinreel Campground. The channel swings north, where you may encounter strong winds head-on in summer.

The creek turns west, sliding through open dunes, then turns south for over 1 mile. The dunes to the north are closed to vehicles, while to the south you may hear and see all-terrain rigs. There are many sandbars and shallow places to stop and get out.

The river becomes very shallow as it nears the sea, and

you may have to carefully pick your route to avoid getting beached. Low river levels in summer may require you to drag your boat across sandy areas, and you may not be able to actually paddle all the way to the ocean. Be careful! Don't scratch up your boat!

Open sand areas near the mouth are closed to entry by foot March 15 to September 15 to protect the western snowy plover.

## Saunders Lake

**Location:**  About 6 miles north of North Bend.

**Directions:**  From the north end of McCullough Bridge, follow US 101 north 6.5 miles and turn northwest on Saunders Lake Rd., following sign to boat ramp at Sen. Jack Ripper County Park.

**Facilities/Etc:**  Vault toilets, picnic area.

**Launch Site:**  Boat ramp or adjacent grassy area to left of ramp. Also off grassy shoreline in front of picnic area.

**Length:**  4.1 miles (perimeter).

**Time:**  2 hours.

**Precautions:**  Many submerged tree stumps hide in the lake's north end. They may or may not break the surface — it depends on how much water is in the lake — so watch for them! Also for fallen trees along shorelines.

**Details:** This is another pretty dunes-country lake, with a small companion lake and some interesting wetlands. Custom homes ring the lakes. From the boat launch, paddle left around a spit of land, then turn right and go under a railroad bridge. From there, paddle right and follow the lake north, exploring coves on your way to the wetlands. In

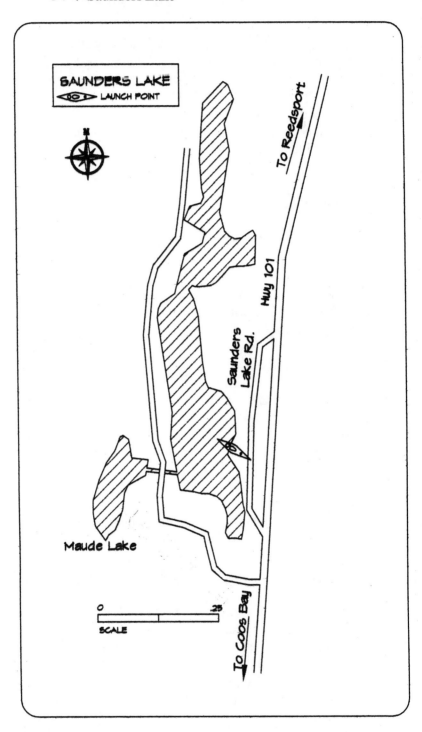

SAUNDERS LAKE
◄◘► LAUNCH POINT

To Reedsport

Hwy 101

Saunders Lake Rd.

Maude Lake

0                    .25
SCALE

To Coos Bay

*Grassy embankment just below the picnic area is a good place to launch into Saunders Lake.*

times of very high water, the lake overflows into Clear Lake, so it might be possible, with caution, to continue a northward paddle. Otherwise, swing southward following the shoreline. On the way back you can check out Maude Lake, under a vehicle bridge to the west.

*Lily pads dot the surface of Beale Lake.*

## Beale Lake

**Location:** 5 miles north of North Bend.

**Directions:** From the north end of McCullough Bridge, follow US 101 about 4 miles and turn west on Hauser Depot Rd. Follow it to a "T" intersection just before the railroad tracks. Turn north and follow the road about 0.5 mile, skirting between railroad tracks and a wood treatment plant. The road turns to gravel and crosses the railroad tracks. Once across the tracks, bear right on a dirt road through towering shrubbery. At the next "Y" intersection is an improvised boat launch at the edge of Beale Lake. The sand/dirt road to the left is for high-clearance 4WD vehicles only, and goes to another lakeside site.

**Facilities/Etc:** None. Very limited parking.

**Launch Site:** Unimproved but easy shrubby/muddy lakeside.

**Length:** 8.1 miles (perimeter).

**Time:** 2 hours

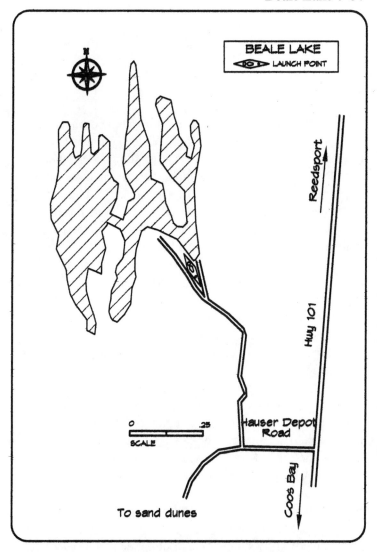

**Precautions:** Strong north winds most summer afternoons can make paddling difficult. As the lake levels lower throughout the summer, more weeds and lily pads appear at or near the surface
.

**Details:** This secluded dunes-country lake is ideal for easy paddling and picnicking. It's actually three long, narrow lakes connected by small channels. Near the west and north parts of the lakes are sand dunes and sandy beaches. Small islands invite exploration.

## Coos Bay Area

The Coos Bay/North Bend area offers some of the south coast's best paddling opportunities. What's variously called Coos Bay, Coos River, or the Coos Bay shipping channel is actually a vast estuary, fed by more than 30 tributaries and covering over 19 square miles of surface area at high tide.

The common denominator throughout the system is the tide. Its reach extends a remarkable *34 miles* up the two main tributaries, the Coos and Millicoma rivers.

The biggest potential problem with sometimes-drastic tides is the danger of getting stranded on mudflats. The mud is soft, sticky and no fun to slog through! You've got to maintain a sense for the main channel, which is usually identified with standard navigational markers.

The good news is that you can also use the tide to your advantage. By planning trips with the changing tides, you can paddle with the tides coming *and* going. Downhill all the way! Or, with a vehicle shuttle, plan more ambitious one-way trips, again utilizing incoming or outgoing tides.

You should obtain a tidebook (available at local stores) and use the corrections, if any, for the places where you're paddling. The daily newspaper also prints tide charts.

When the term "high tide" is used for these tours, it refers to the time of high tide at the Coos Bay channel entrance/ocean beaches.

As you go "upriver," the time of high tide time is later respective to how far upriver you travel. I've noted the approximate corrections for high tide or low tide at various places, but land observations should always be made prior to paddling. Currents are another factor, since they don't correspond with the actual high and low tide times. See information in the Introduction.

Wind is also an important influence. *There are strong north winds during most summer afternoons*, while in winter, storms blow in from the south.

The Coos estuary is accessible in dozens of places, from official boat ramps and docks to undeveloped put-ins and beaches. You can make out-and-back trips, or use a vehicle shuttle for longer excursions.

If you're not comfortable crossing the bay, you can follow the shoreline, or consider launching from one of the sites that offer access to islands in the bay.

The first tours discuss trips in the main channel, from Charleston "upriver" past Empire, North Bend, Coos Bay, Eastside and up the Coos and Millicoma rivers.

The later sections deal with the inlets and sloughs of the Coos Bay estuary, including the South Slough National Estuarine Research Reserve.

Approximate tide time corrections for Coos Bay Area:
Empire Boat Ramp: +40 minutes.
Railroad Bridge: +1 hour
California Street (North Bend) Boat Ramp: +1 hour 10 minutes
Downtown Coos Bay: +1 hour 25 minutes
Eastside Boat Ramp: +1 hour 35 minutes

## Charleston Harbor to Empire Boat Ramp

**Location:** About 12 miles southwest of Coos Bay/North Bend.

**Directions:** From US 101 in North Bend or Coos Bay, follow signs to Charleston, Ocean Beaches, State Parks. The roads eventually lead to Coos Bay's Empire district. Follow the main route (Newmark St.) as it heads west toward the edge of the Coos Bay channel. At the foot of Newmark St. is the Empire Boat Ramp. The main route to Charleston (Empire Blvd., aka Charleston Hwy) swings south, and follows near the shoreline to Charleston. Cross the bridge over South Slough and turn north on Boat Basin

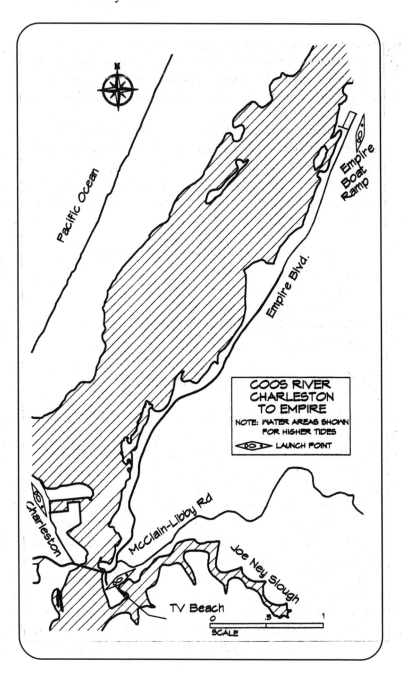

Pacific Ocean

Empire Boat Ramp

Empire Blvd.

COOS RIVER
CHARLESTON
TO EMPIRE
NOTE: WATER AREAS SHOWN
FOR HIGHER TIDES
◁○▷ LAUNCH POINT

Charleston

McClain-Libby Rd

Joe Ney Slough

TV Beach

0        .5        1
SCALE

Drive, and continue north to the public boat ramps.
*Alternate launch*: Just before Charleston Bridge, turn
south on Troller Rd. and continue 2 blocks to parking area
marked by sign for Distant Water Fleet Facility. It's sometimes called TV Beach because a paddler once noticed a
TV set in the mud there, and later removed it for recycling.

**Facilities/Etc:** Restrooms, showers, full services in
Charleston.

**Launch Site:** Public boat ramps or docks in Charleston
marina. Sandy beach at Troller Rd. (TV Beach) launch
site.

**Length:** 3.7 miles one way.

**Time:** 2 hours.

**Precautions:** Watch for swells coming in from channel
entrance in vicinity of north and south jetties. Watch for
fishing, shipping and recreational boats, and for floats
attached to which are ropes securing crab pots. Wind and
floating logs can also be a hazard. Water is shallow along
eastern shoreline of channel.

**Details:** Because of wind, ocean swells and the exposed
nature of this part of the bay, this isn't among my favorite
paddles, but under the right conditions, it can be interesting.
It also keeps you on one side of the channel if you're
hesitant about crossing the bay.

Launch on an incoming tide from the Charleston docks or
boat ramp and swing north out of the harbor, staying along
the eastern shore. You'll pass Pigeon Point and a small
island that is sometimes home to sea lions. Another high-
light is the long-abandoned Coos Head sawmill and its old
decaying pier.

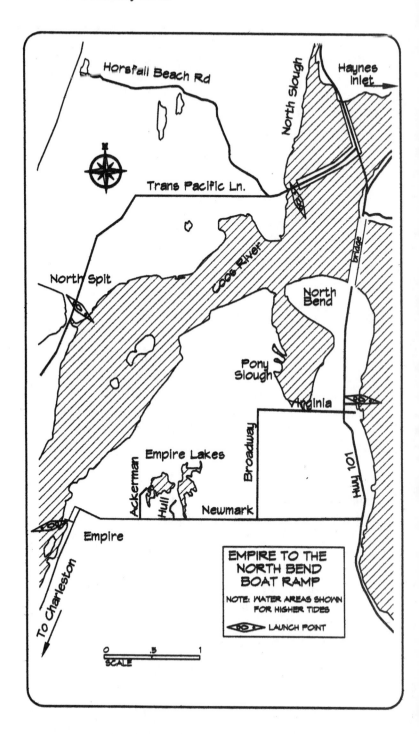

# Empire to North Spit Launch Point

**Location:** 5 miles west of Coos Bay/North Bend.

**Directions:** From US 101 in North Bend or Coos Bay, follow signs to Charleston, Ocean Beaches, State Parks. The roads eventually lead to Coos Bay's Empire district. Follow the main route (Newmark St.) as it heads west toward the edge of the Coos Bay channel. At the foot of Newmark St. is Empire Boat Ramp.

**Facilities/Etc:** Improved restrooms, picnic tables, boat launch, fishing dock.

**Launch Site:** Public boat launch or beach area at south end of parking lot.

**Length:** 2.7 miles.

**Time:** 1+ hour. High tide at Empire is 40 minutes later than high tide at Coos Bay channel entrance/ocean beaches.

**Precautions:** This paddle involves a channel crossing. Use caution at all times and do not attempt during storms or heavy chop. Watch for shipping traffic.

**Details:** One of several excursions possible from the Empire Boat Ramp, this tour takes you to a sandy beach over on the North Spit. You could also use this as a jumping-off point to explore islands in the bay, or to continue to other destinations listed in the next tours.

## North Spit Boat Ramp

**Location:** North Spit of Coos Bay Estuary, about 10 miles west of Coos Bay/North Bend.

**Directions:** From the north end of McCullough Bridge,

*A row of pilings breaks the wave action near the
Bureau of Land Management North Spit Boat Ramp.
You can launch several expeditions from here.*

follow US 101 north 0.6 mile and turn west on Trans
Pacific Ln., following signs to Oregon Dunes, Horsfall
Beach. Follow road across causeway. At a "Y" intersection, bear left on Trans Pacific Ln., following signs to BLM
boat ramp.

**Facilities/Etc:**  Improved restrooms, picnic tables.

**Launch Site:**  Boat ramp, dock, sandy beach.

**Length:**  6 miles roundtrip.

**Time:** 3+ hours, with time for land-based exploration.

**Precautions:** Use caution when entering bay waters and do not launch during storms or heavy chop. Watch for shipping traffic. Tidal current is strong; consult tide charts!

**Details:** Use BLM North Spit Boat Ramp to launch tide-assisted excursions in the bay to visit dredge spoils islands or just cruise along coves and small inlets. Another potential outing begins on the later stages of an outgoing tide: Paddle "downriver" (toward the ocean) on the north side of the channel. You'll pass several dredge spoils islands that invite exploration. In about 3 miles are old pilings where Navy minesweepers once tied up. You can beach here and explore abandoned World War II ammo bunkers and Coast Guard building sites. Then use the incoming tide to help your return to the launch site.

## North Spit launch point to California Street Boat Ramp (North Bend)

**Location:** About 3 miles north of North Bend.

**Details:** From north end of McCullough Bridge, continue north on US 101 0.6 mile and turn west on Trans Pacific Ln., following signs to Oregon Dunes, Horsfall Beach. At west end of causeway the road crosses a bridge. Immediately across bridge, make a U-turn and park on south edge of road. Directly below is a small sandy beach from which you can launch.

**Facilities/Etc:** none.

**Launch Site:** Sandy beach.

**Length:** 2.3 miles one way

**Precautions:** This paddle requires a channel crossing. Use caution when entering bay waters and do not launch during storms or heavy chop. Watch for shipping traffic.

**Discussion:** This is yet another potential tour of the lower bay, with highlights that include passage under the swing-span railroad bridge and the soaring green girders of McCullough Bridge. You can also explore Pony Slough (see next tour for more details.) You'll go around the "north bend" that gives the city its name, and pass along part of the working waterfront before arriving at California Street Boat Ramp.

# Pony Slough

**Location:** On the Coos River channel west of McCullough Bridge and the swing-span railroad bridge. This is the body of water across from Pony Village Mall in North Bend.

**Directions:** You can launch from the California Street Boat Ramp in North Bend, or from an unimproved shore-line site in North Bend, or from the North Spit launch point across the channel.

*North Spit launch point*: From the north end of McCullough Bridge, head north on US 101 for 0.6 mile and turn west on Trans Pacific Ln., following signs to Oregon Dunes and Horsfall Beach. Drive across the causeway, which crosses a small bridge at its west end. Immediately across the bridge, make a U-turn and park on the south edge of the road. Directly below is a small sandy beach from which you can launch.
*California St. Boat Ramp:* From US 101 northbound or southbound in North Bend, turn east on California Ave. and follow it to edge of bay.
*Alternate Launch Site:* For a shorter trip or to avoid paddling around North Point and under McCullough Bridge or across the river, turn west off US 101 on Florida Ave.

and follow it to the edge of Pony Slough. Launching here should be done at or near high tide.

**Facilities/Etc:** Improved restrooms at California Street Boat Ramp.

**Launch Site:** See directions above.

**Length:** 3 miles depending upon launch site.

**Time:** 1.5 hours

**Precautions:** Strong north winds can make the slough quite rough. Don't get caught out on a falling tide. *Paddle only at or near high tide as this area is mostly mudflats during low tide!*

**Details:** This slough, at high tide, is a glittering expanse of water that serves as home and resting place for a wide variety of birds. The North Bend Airport borders the western shore, but the rest of the slough has been left in its natural state. The sandy shoreline near the railroad bridge is strewn with shells. At the southern end is Pony Creek, up which you can paddle a short distance depending on the tide.

From the California Street Boat Ramp, paddle north around Simpson Heights, under McCullough Bridge and the railroad bridge. Just past the railroad bridge turn south into Pony Slough. Watch for shallow sections along the margins. If you put in at the North Spit launch site, you'll have to paddle across the main channel. Paddle around the edges watching for shallow areas. Launching from the North Spit launch point will require paddling across the river.

# North Bend to Coos Bay

**Location:** Near downtown North Bend, just east of US 101.

*With the Coos Bay waterfront as a backdrop, a paddler makes her way toward the Eastside Boat Ramp.*

**Directions:** From US 101 in North Bend, turn east on California Ave. and follow it to the edge of channel.

**Facilities/Etc:** Improved restrooms, boat ramp, dock.

**Length:** 2 miles one way.

**Time:** 1 hour. High tide at California Street Boat Ramp is 1 hour 10 minutes later than high tide at channel entrance/ocean beaches.

**Launch Site:** Boat ramp, dock.

**Precautions:** Be aware of shallow water, and be alert about the tides, as an outgoing tide may strand you in shallow muddy areas. Keep well back from passing commercial boats and ships.

**Details:** You can paddle up the channel to Coos Bay, passing the Mill Casino. There's a little beach at the south end of the casino's waterfront boardwalk at which you can pull up, with stairs leading to the parking lot. Beyond the casino is other waterfront development, including docks at which ships, barges and tugs are moored. Paddle along the Coos Bay Boardwalk and the public docks. You can potentially stop at the docks, but they're somewhat high out

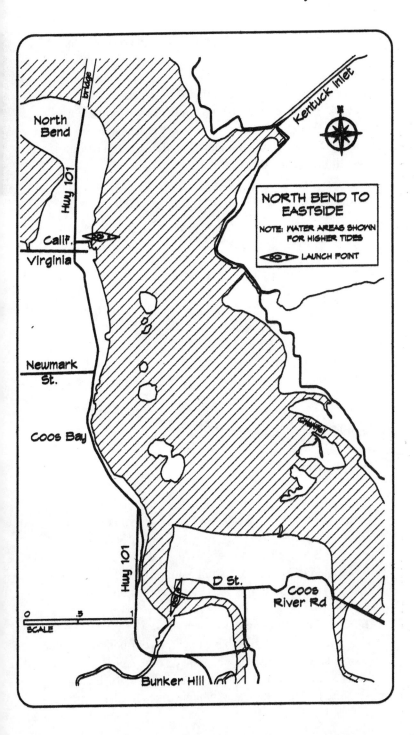

of the water, making it difficult to get in and out of your craft.

From California Street Boat Ramp you can also launch trips to the east side of the bay (1.6 mile one-way to Kentuck Inlet), or to the islands in the bay. There are a number of potential landing spots on the east shores of the islands. Or, paddle down-channel to McCullough Bridge, Pony Slough, and other destinations.

## Coos Bay to Eastside Boat Ramp

**Location:** Downtown Coos Bay

**Directions:** Follow US 101 to downtown Coos Bay. The Coos Bay Boardwalk is parallel to northbound US 101 (Bayshore Drive), with the main entrance at the foot of Anderson St.

**Facilities/Etc:** Improved restrooms at Bay Area Information Center office across from city dock and at Eastside Boat Ramp.

**Launch Site:** Public boat docks.

**Length:** 1 mile

**Time:** 1 hour. High tide at Coos Bay docks is 1 hour 25 minutes later than high tide at Coos Bay channel entrance/ ocean beaches.

**Precautions:** Watch for fishing, shipping and recreational boats. Wind and floating logs can also be a hazard.

**Details:** This is a potential launch; however, it has a couple of problems: First, you'll have to carry your boat from your vehicle across railroad tracks, go up some stairs, over the docks and down a narrow gangplank. Secondly, the docks are quite high off the water, which makes it difficult to get in and out of your craft. From here you can paddle over to the Eastside Boat Ramp, or to other destinations discussed in the previous and upcoming tours.

## Eastside to Coos and Millicoma Rivers

**Location:** Eastside Boat Ramp is approximately 3 miles east (by road) of Coos Bay; other boat ramps are at various locations upriver.

**Directions:**
**Eastside Boat Ramp**: From US 101 at the south end of Coos Bay, follow signs to Allegany, Coos River. Cross Isthmus Slough Bridge and bear left on 6th Ave, following it north 0.5 mile to "T" intersection with D St. Turn west on D St. and follow it to Eastside Boat Ramp.
**Doris Place Boat Ramp (Millicoma River)**: Follow directions above to "T" intersection in Eastside. Turn east on Coos River Rd. and follow it 2.3 miles to Chandler Bridge. Cross bridge, following signs to Allegany. In 1.7 miles turn north on access road to boat ramp.
**Rooke-Higgins County Park Boat Ramp (Millicoma River)**: Follow directions above to Doris Place Boat Ramp and continue upriver 4.5 miles and turn west into boat ramp area.
**Myrtle Tree Boat Ramp (Coos River)**: Follow directions above to "T" intersection in Eastside. Turn east on Coos River Rd. and follow it 2.3 miles to Chandler Bridge. Do not cross bridge; continue on south bank road, following signs to Coos River Learning Center, Dellwood. Boat ramp is 4.5 miles upriver from Chandler Bridge.

**Facilities/Etc:** Vault toilets at all boat ramps. Picnicking and camping at Rooke-Higgins.

**Launch Sites:** Boat ramps, grassy embankments.

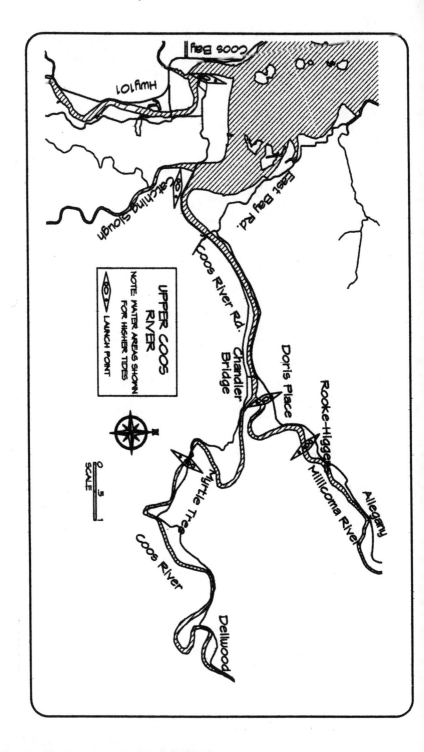

Photo by Iain D.P. Karroll

*Paddlers enjoy a leisurely day on the Coos River near Myrtle Tree Boat Ramp. This is still part of the Coos estuary, so be mindful of tide times and currents.*

**Length:** Eastside Boat Ramp to:

Coos Bay waterfront: 0.4 mile

Catching Slough Bridge: 3.1 miles

Forks of rivers: 7.7 miles

Doris Place ramp (Millicoma River): 7.8 miles

Rooke-Higgins ramp (Millicoma): 11.2 miles

Allegany/West Fork (tidewater): 16.1 miles

Myrtle Tree ramp (Coos River): 10 miles

Dellwood (Coos River tidewater): 18 miles

**Time:** Varies depending on length of trip, currents and tide. High tide at Eastside Boat Ramp is 1 hour 35 minutes later than channel entrance/ocean beaches.

**Precautions:** Be aware of tide times and plan trips accordingly. Low tides reveal shallow, muddy areas. In all exposed channels of the Coos Bay estuary, strong northerly winds can build up adverse wave conditions in the afternoons of summer and fall.

**Details:** A number of out-and-back treks are possible, as well as shuttle-assisted treks. Trips should utilize tides. The upper reaches of the Coos and Millicoma rivers are quite beautiful, but most of the riverside is private property, with few places except public boat ramps to launch or get out. The rivers yield few sand bars, gravel bars or easy places to land.

During most of the year, tidal influences affect currents as far as 30 miles up both rivers, but in winter and spring after heavy rainfall, river current can prevail over tidal influences at upriver locations.

Head of tidewater on the Millicoma River is near the settlement of Allegany. In times of high water it's possible to paddle about a mile farther. The Coos River's tidewater ends around Dellwood, which is the entrance to Weyerhaeuser's Millicoma Tree Farm. Here again, it's possible to paddle farther when river levels permit in winter and early spring.

## Coos Bay Area Inlets and Sloughs

As discussed in the previous section, the Coos estuary includes more than three dozen tidal arms, many of which offer excellent paddling. One of them takes in the South Slough National Estuarine Research Reserve, which has the distinction of being the nation's first such preserve. Others have adjacent marshes protected from development.

The tidal arms are often – and quite correctly – called sloughs, although early-day community boosters preferred the term *inlet*, thinking the word slough too dismal and swampy-sounding.

Thus the seeming-contradiction at times over such place names as Pony *Slough* and Haynes *Inlet*.

## North Slough (Hauser Channel)

**Location:** 1 mile north of McCullough Bridge.

**Directions:** From McCullough Bridge, head north on US 101 for 0.6 mile and turn west on Trans Pacific Ln., following signs to Oregon Dunes and Horsfall Beach. Drive across the causeway, which crosses a bridge at its west end. Immediately across the bridge, make a U-turn and park on the south edge of the road. Directly below is a small sandy beach. This launch site can also be used for paddling Haynes Inlet or into the Coos Bay channel.

**Facilities/Etc:** None.

**Launch Site:** Small sandy beach.

**Length:** 7.1 miles round trip

**Time:** 3+ hours

**Precautions:** Submerged pilings. Pay close attention to tides and don't get stranded on a falling tide.

**Details:** Great wetlands paddle. Many birds including eagles, egrets, and herons can be observed. Begin your paddle at approximately the time listed in tide charts for high tide at the Coos Bay channel entrance/ocean beaches, and you will have the incoming tide with you. (See page 2 for important notes about tide times.) Paddle under the vehicle bridge adjacent to the put-in beach and head north.

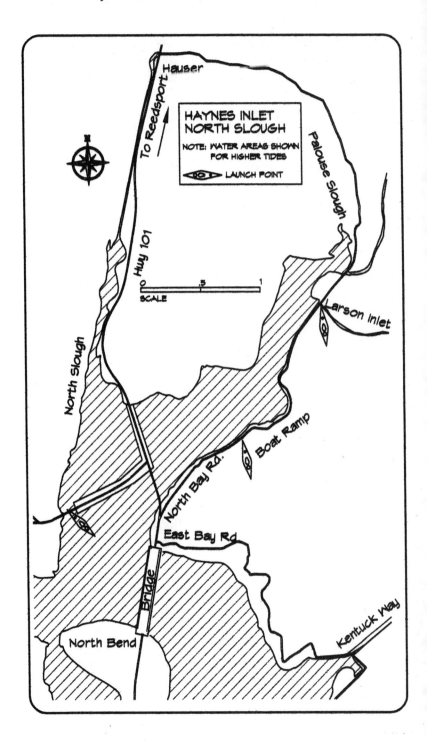

Stay to the west edge of the slough as you go north, paddling over shallow water. Continue north. The waterway narrows. Once past the narrow section, begin to head east toward US 101. The main channel parallels US 101. You can explore the wetlands away from the channel *but beware of being caught out on a falling tide.* Continue to paddle north until you come to the bridge and tidegate under US 101. If you've timed your trip correctly, the tide will have changed as you reach the turn-around point, and you'll have the outgoing current for your return.

## Haynes Inlet

**Location/Directions/Launch site/Facilities:** See previous tour.

**Alternate launch site**: 0.2 mile north of McCullough Bridge on US 101, turn east on North Bay Rd. and continue about 1 mile to a boat ramp just before the Clausen Oyster plant. Follow information in previous chapter on North Slough for location, directions and launch site.

**Length:** 8 miles if you paddle the perimeter of the inlet.

**Time:** Approximately 3 hours.

**Precautions:** All of this paddle is within a part of the bay greatly influenced by tides, with shallow water and mudflats on the margins. Paddling on the incoming tide should allow you to safely travel the area. Various navigational signs mark the main channel. Strong wind can be focused around the Haynes Inlet Bridge. Watch for oyster harvesting and fishing boats. All oyster beds are private property, so no poaching!

**Details:** Beautiful backwater of the bay, rich with wildlife and birds. Launch at the time listed for high tide at channel entrance/ocean beaches. (See important note about tides on page 2.) If possible, paddle in the morning when winds are likely to be at a minimum. Paddle west, parallel to the causeway, toward US 101 and Haynes Inlet Bridge. Paddle under the bridge. The current will be strongest here, due to narrowing of the inlet. If the expected tide is reasonably high, you can turn left after paddling under the bridge and explore this part of the slough. Paddle north, parallel to US 101, until you reach the northern shore, then follow the shoreline east.

At the extreme eastern end of Haynes Inlet is Palouse Creek. Depending upon tide height, you can paddle up this creek. After paddling the creek and returning to Haynes Inlet, continue along the southern shoreline, paddling west to your starting point.

Along the way you'll pass Lone Rock, a small, picturesque island. North Bay Rd. runs along the shoreline, and there's a boat ramp just west of an oyster processing plant. Depending upon tide heights, you'll also see a couple of sandy beaches if you want to get out of your boat.

## Larson Slough

**Location:** About 2 miles from North Bend.

**Directions:** From McCullough Bridge, follow US 101 north about 0.2 mile, and turn east on North Bay Rd. In 2.5 miles turn south on Larson Ln. and park near bridge tidegate.

**Facilities/Etc:** None.

**Launch Site:** Next to bridge at intersection of Larson Ln. and North Bay Rd.

**Length:** 5 miles if the tide is quite high, or if heavy rainfall has recently occurred.

**Time:** 2 hours.

**Precautions:** Shallow water. Beware of being left stranded in later stages of outgoing tide.

**Details:** Very narrow, winding paddle through a small valley. Peaceful countryside, with cattle ranches lining the route and lots of birdlife. The channel narrows into shallow, reedy wetlands.

Launch 1.5 hours before time listed on tide charts for high tide at Coos Bay channel entrance/ocean beaches. (See important note about tides on page 2.) You'll have the incoming tide with you as you head upchannel, and an outgoing tide for your return.

## South Slough Area

Coos Bay's South Slough encompasses several branches of its own, including Joe Ney Slough and the two arms of the South Slough National Estuarine Research Reserve. You can start expeditions in several places. Launch out-and-back trips from Charleston, exploring the shoreline and visiting Valino Island, a 23-acre island within the research reserve. Or launch out-and-back paddles from the Hinch Ln. put-in. Best of all is to plan a vehicle shuttle.

*Be sure to account for the tide as you could be caught out in the mud on a falling tide in the distant reaches of South Slough.*

**Location:** About 12 miles west of Coos Bay/North Bend.

**Directions:** From US 101 in North Bend or Coos Bay, follow signs to State Parks, Ocean Beaches, Charleston. You'll eventually end up on Newmark St.; follow it west near the edge of the bay, then swing south as the road becomes S. Empire Blvd., following signs to Charleston. Once in Charleston, there are two potential put-ins.
**Troller Rd. put-in (TV Beach):** Just before crossing Charleston Bridge, turn south on Troller Rd. and follow it several blocks to a parking area just before the gates to the

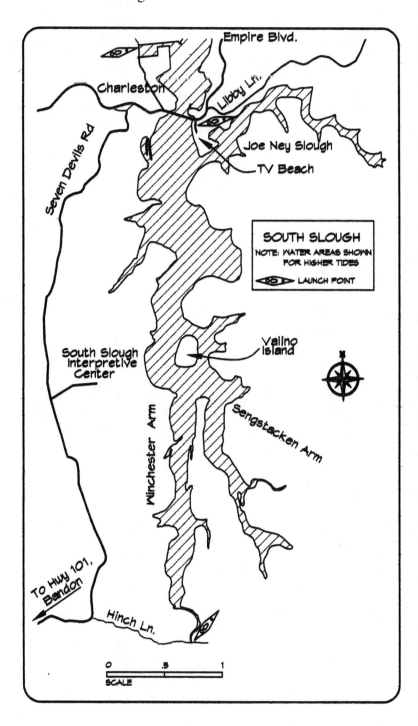

Port of Coos Bay shipyards. A sign identifies this as the Distant Water Fleet Facility.

**Charleston Harbor Boat Ramp**: Follow directions above, and cross the Charleston Bridge. One block past the bridge turn north on Boat Basin Way and follow signs to boat ramp.

**Hinch Ln. put-in**: Follow directions above and proceed over Charleston Bridge and through Charleston. Just beyond Charleston turn south on Seven Devils Rd., and follow it 5.3 miles to Hinch Ln., marked by a South Slough National Estuarine Research Reserve sign. Follow gravel Hinch Ln. to the edge of slough.

**Facilities/Etc:** Improved restrooms and showers near Charleston Boat Ramp. Improved restrooms and showers at Port of Coos Bay shipyard on Troller Rd. Rv parks, campgrounds and other services in Charleston.

**Launch sites:** See directions above.

**Length:** Troller Rd. put-in to Hinch Ln. take-out: 4+ miles one-way if you take a direct route; longer if you paddle all the shoreline.

**Time:** 2.5 hours minimum. Longer if you explore all the available area.

**Precautions:** Watch for shallow areas. In the summer the north wind can be quite strong, resulting in very rough water conditions, particularly when combined with strong tides. Plan your trip for in the morning, if possible. Winter storms can bring strong south wind. The first part of the paddle is more exposed than the last half.

**Details:** Established in 1975 as the nation's first estuarine reserve, the South Slough National Estuarine Research Reserve is comprised of 4,700 acres, 700 of which are

*Kayakers paddle toward a take-out at the grassy embankments at Hinch Lane in the South Slough National Estuarine Research Reserve.*

tidelands and freshwater marshes. The reserve also features a 23-acre island. Birdlife is abundant, and this is one of the premier paddles in the region. The South Slough Reserve's interpretive center (PO Box 5417, Charleston OR 97420, 541-888-5558) has a paddling brochure, and also has guided paddle tours in the summer.

It's best to paddle on an incoming tide. The usual tour is to paddle from Charleston to the Hinch Ln. take-out, using a vehicle shuttle.

Valino Island is located about 2.2 miles from the Charleston launch site. This island had early settlers' homes. A little south of Valino Island, stay to the west and paddle into Winchester Arm.

It's easy to paddle into dead-end areas, so be prepared to turn around and paddle back out and into the main channel.

**Sengstacken Arm**: If you paddle to the east from Valino Island, you'll enter Sengstacken Arm, which has no-take out area to allow for a vehicle shuttle, but is perhaps the best and most interesting part of South Slough. Begin this paddle from the Troller Rd. put-in, about 1.5 hours before high tide. Paddle south toward Valino Island. If it is building to a fairly high tide, you can paddle around the east side of the island. The deepest part of the channel is toward the east side. Otherwise, paddle around the island on its west side.

After rounding the island, paddle toward the east and into Sengstacken Arm. Continue south. Paddling to the extreme end will bring you to the junction of John's Creek (3.3 miles from Troller Rd. put-in) and Talbot Creek. If it is a fairly high tide, you may be able to paddle up John's Creek for some distance. It narrows to a channel of about 15 to 20 feet. The distance to this point from the put-in is 3.8 miles. At the junction, paddling east will take you up Talbot Creek for approximately 0.5 mile depending upon tide heights. The most interesting side trip would be to paddle through the notch into Elliot Creek. Once through the notch, the creek widens into another small bay. The channel is to the right. Paddling to the end will bring you to a tidegate. Paddling all the creeks and returning to the Troller Rd. put-in would give you a total distance of approximately 10 miles.

The Cape Arago Audubon Society's *Birding the Southern Oregon Coast* suggests that you might see sharp-shinned hawk, white-tailed kite and red-tailed hawk hunting from snags, while rufous hummingbird, marsh wren and violet-green swallow are among many of the birds commonly seen in the meadows in summer.

**Precautions:** Strong north winds could make paddling back to your starting point difficult. Be sure to consult tide table and paddle only on an incoming tide. Getting caught out on a falling tide will result in being stuck in the mud.

**Hinch Ln. put-in/take-out:** In years past, it was possible to paddle south (upstream) for nearly 1 mile from the Hinch Ln. launch site, but a tree blocks the way. The channel is narrow, winding and very interesting.

## Joe Ney Slough

**Location/Directions/Facilities/Launch Site:** See previous tour and launch from the Troller Rd. (TV Beach) site.

**Length:** 3.2 miles round trip

**Time:** 2+ hours

**Precautions:** Beware of shallow areas on an outgoing tide. These shallow areas are basically mudflats. Do not disturb commercial oyster beds.

**Details:** This is a winding, mellow paddle in protected waters. From the Troller Rd. launch site, paddle south and turn left around the boat yard into Joe Ney Slough. Going right takes you into the South Slough area. Many birds are present. You also paddle through private oyster beds. The tour ends at an earthen dam that impounds water in a reservoir for the Coos Bay area's water system. There's an interesting fish ladder. If you launch just before high tide, you will be able to use the current to your advantage, and you will be able to explore a larger area.

# Coalbank Slough

**Location:** South end of Coos Bay.

**Directions:** From south end of Coos Bay on US 101, follow sign to Allegany. Cross Isthmus Slough Bridge and bear left on 6th Ave, following it north 0.5 mile to "T" intersection with D St. Turn west on D St. and follow it to Eastside Boat Ramp.

**Facilities/Etc:** Vault toilets, picnic tables at Eastside Boat Ramp.

**Launch Site:** Boat ramp/dock at Eastside Boat Ramp. *Alternate launch site*: Directly below the US 101 bridge over Coalbank Slough, you can launch from a sandy beach. Roads from the bridge's east end leads to the beach. *Alternate launch site:* Two blocks east of US 101 bridge over Coalbank Slough, turn south on Harriet Rd. In 2 blocks turn west on Coal Bank Ln. and follow it 0.3 mile to intersection with Broadway Rd. Boat ramp is along channel bank, just past "Dead End" sign.

**Length:** 5 miles paddling from the Eastside Boat Ramp.

**Time:** 2 hours. High tide at the entrance to Coalbank Slough is about 1.5 hours after high tide at Coos Bay channel entrance/ocean beaches.

**Precautions:** Use caution crossing the bay and do not launch during storms or heavy chop. Watch for shipping traffic. Paddle on incoming tide. Watch for submerged debris at the end of the slough.

**Details:** This slough wanders southwest through Coos Bay's Englewood district, ending in the Libby area. You slip through protected wetlands, with areas where waterfowl nest right along the shoreline, while other sections are lined with industrial development, homes and ranches. The channel ends at a dike and tidegate.

## Catching Slough

**Location:** Approximately 5 miles east of the city of Coos Bay.

*Few places in the Coos Bay area so dramatically illustrate the effects of tidal extremes as Catching Slough. These photos, taken at the eastern end of Catching Slough Bridge at typical high and low tides, show what a difference a few hours make.*

**Directions:** From the south end of Coos Bay on US 101, follow signs to Allegany, Coos River. Follow the road across Isthmus Slough Bridge, then swing north, following signs to Allegany, Catching Slough. Continue north 0.5 mile to a "T" intersection and turn east, following signs to Allegany and Catching Slough. In 1.1 miles the road crosses Catching Slough Bridge. Just across the bridge,

*At high tide (photo this page), water laps right to the edge of an unimproved boat ramp, but at low tide (photo on opposite page), the channel is several hundred feet away -- through sticky mud. Don't get caught!*

turn south on Catching Slough Rd. and park in area below bridge.

**Facilities/Etc:** None

**Launch Site:** Boat ramp at east end of bridge.

**Length:** 8+ mile round trip.

**Time:** 3+ hours.

**Precautions:** Debris, limbs and other floating items especially after heavy rains.

**Details:** Winding paddle through farmland and wooded areas. Consider the tide when launching. If you plan to paddle to the end and back, try to start about 2 hours before high tide at Coos Bay channel entrance/ocean beaches, and use the incoming current to take you up slough.

## Isthmus Slough

Isthmus Slough reaches out from the south end of the Coos Bay estuary, twisting about 10 miles and branching out into a couple of interesting little side-sloughs before ending at a tidegate near the settlement of Greenacres. It was an important pioneer waterway, and decaying remnants remain from that era, many visible only from the water.

You can access Isthmus Slough from Coos Bay's main channel, or begin your explorations at put-ins along the slough. Use the tides to your advantage when exploring Isthmus Slough; be sure to consult tide tables. I've provided the tide differentials for each put-in.

Consider a vehicle shuttle if you're planning a full paddle of Isthmus Slough. Also remember that this is a working waterway for the wood industry, so be aware of tugboats, barges and log rafts. Incidentally, log rafts tend to concen-

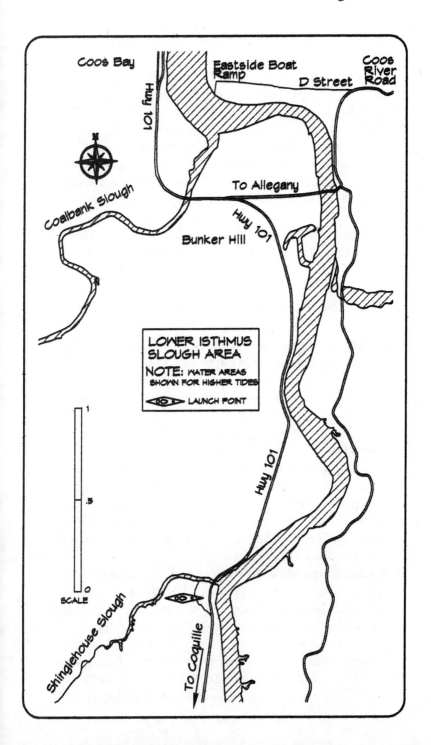

trate currents, since they force a narrowing of the channel in places.

Isthmus Slough holds many traces of the region's history. A tiny inlet along the way is the final resting place of an old boat — watch for its distinctive "bare bones." At Southport are crumbling old docks, and near Davis Slough are the remains of coal barges and other watercraft. Pioneer-era railroads ran over and alongside the sloughs on wooden trestles still visible today, while pilings and foundations of old towns can be found on the east side of the slough.

From Isthmus Slough, three sloughs branch off. They are shorter paddles and can easily be done on a round-trip basis. They should all be done at or near high tide.

## Eastside Boat Ramp to Isthmus Slough

**Location:** Eastside Boat Ramp is about 3 miles east (by land) from downtown Coos Bay. Other Isthmus Slough boat ramps and a put-in are located along US 101 at various points for approximately 10 miles south of Coos Bay.

**Directions:**
**Eastside Boat Ramp**: From "Y" intersection at the south end of Coos Bay on US 101, go east, following sign to Allegany, Coos River. Cross Isthmus Slough Bridge and bear left on 6th Ave, following it north 0.5 mile to "T" intersection with D St. Turn west on D St. and follow it to Eastside Boat Ramp.
**Shinglehouse Slough Boat Ramp**: From south end of Coos Bay on US 101, go south on US 101. In about 2.3 miles US 101 crosses a low bridge over Coalbank Slough. About 200 feet south, just past MP 242 marker, turn right into access road.
**Davis Slough launch site:** From south end of Coos Bay on US 101, go south on US 101 about 4.5 miles to "Y" junction of US 101 and Highway 42, and take Highway 42.

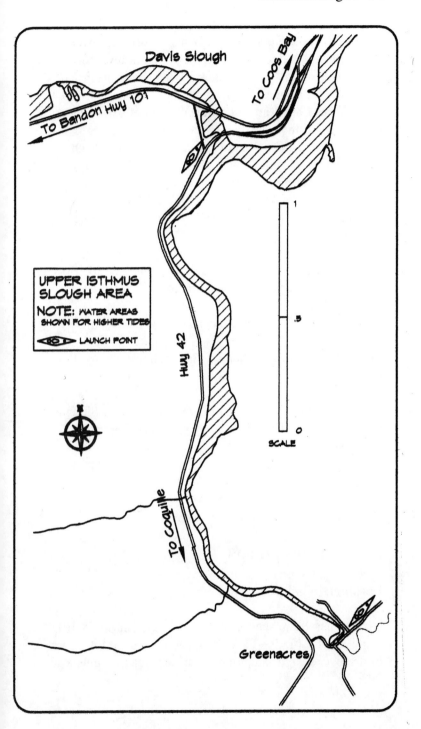

In about .05 mile the highway crosses a low bridge over Davis Slough. In a few hundred feet, turn northwest on connector road to US 101. Launch from grassy areas and embankments adjacent to this road.

**Greenacres Boat Ramp**: From south end of Coos Bay on US 101, go south on US 101 approximately 4.5 miles to "Y" junction of US 101 and Highway 42, and take Highway 42 about 3.2 miles (7.7 miles total from Coos Bay) to Greenacres exit. Follow Greenacres Rd. down to and across railroad tracks. Bear left at "Y" intersection and continue about 300 feet and turn into boat ramp parking area.

**Facilities/Etc:** Vault toilets, picnic tables at Eastside Boat Ramp. No facilities at other boat ramps or launch site.

**Launch Sites:** Boat ramps, docks, grassy embankments.

**Length:** Eastside Boat Ramp to Shinglehouse Slough Boat Ramp: 3.1 miles. High tide at Eastside Boat Ramp +1 hour 35 minutes.

Shinglehouse Slough Boat Ramp to Davis Slough put-in: 3.2 hours. High tide at Davis Slough +2 hours 30 minutes.

Davis Slough put-in to Greenacres Boat Ramp: 2.7 miles High tide at Greenacres +3 hours.

**Precautions:** See discussion above.

# Shinglehouse Slough

**Location:** 3 miles south of Coos Bay.

**Directions:** From south end of Coos Bay, follow US 101 south about 2.1 miles. Pass Shinglehouse Slough Rd., cross bridge over slough and turn into parking area near milepost 242.

**Facilities/Etc:** None

**Launch Site:** A public boat ramp is located on the south-west side to the highway. From here, you can paddle Shinglehouse Slough or out into Isthmus Slough.

**Length:** 2 miles round trip

**Time:** 1 hour. High tide at the entrance of this slough is

*Amidst the peaceful reaches of Davis Slough.*

approximately 2 hours later than high tide at channel entrance/ocean beaches.

**Precautions:** Old wood pilings line one side of the slough; some are partially submerged.

**Details:** Relatively short paddle. More area is available at high tides levels. The channel narrows and becomes a shallow, reedy area.

# Davis Slough

**Location:** 5 miles south of Coos Bay at the junction of US 101 and Highway 42.

**Directions:** From Coos Bay, go south on US 101 approximately 4.5 miles to "Y" junction of US 101 and Highway 42, and take Highway 42. Just past bridge over Davis Slough, turn northwest on connector road that leads back to US 101.

**Facilities/Etc:** None.

**Launch Site:** Launch only at or near high tide. Launch from site along connector road that links Highway 42 and US 101. (See map) Here you'll find a triangle of water between two bridges. At high tide, you can launch from a grassy area, but as the tide falls, this will become a fairly steep mud bank.
**Length:** 2.8 miles

**Time:** 1+ hour. High tide is approximately 3 hours later than channel entrance/ocean beaches.

**Precautions:** Lots of old pilings. At very high tides, you may not be able to paddle under the bridges.
**Details:** Paddle under US 101 bridge and head west. The slough splits into two parts. The left channel parallels US

101, with sections of old logging train trestles visible, and ends at a culvert. The right channel opens into wider wetlands that can be paddled at higher tides, and ends at a diked embankment. The area available to paddle is greatly dependent on the height of the tide.

## John Topits Park/Empire Lakes

**Location:** In Coos Bay's Empire District, approximately 5 miles from downtown Coos Bay.

**Directions:** From downtown Coos Bay go north on US 101 1.7 miles and turn west on Newmark St. In 1.8 miles turn north on Hull St., following sign to John Topits Park/ Middle Lake. (John Topits Park/Lower Lake access is three blocks west on Newmark St.) (See map page 62.)

**Facilities/Etc:** Vault toilets at Middle Lake. Improved restrooms at Lower Lake.

**Launch Site:** Boat ramps or sandy beaches.

*Serene, forested setting of Empire Lakes belie their proximity to the busy Coos Bay area.*

**Length:** 3 miles (combined perimeters)

**Time:** 2 hours

**Precautions:** Lots of trees, stumps and limbs in the water

**Details:** Lazy paddle in a very picturesque sheltered area. Birdlife abounds, and the lakes are stocked with fish. Good place to practice kayak Eskimo rolls and safety techniques but be aware of water quality. Upper/Middle Lake borders Southwestern Oregon Community College. There's an extensive trail system around the lakes.

## Coquille River

The Coquille River as it nears the Pacific Ocean offers another of the coast's interesting estuaries, with tidal influence reaching as far as 30 miles upriver. Paddling opportunities abound, with treks that pass by historic townsites, old abandoned boats, Indian fish weirs and a national wildlife refuge. Most of the riverbank is private property, but there are eight launch sites from the river's outlet at Bandon to the inland town of Myrtle Point. The most scenic trips utilize the tides in the downriver sections and include a loop trip around Randolph Island. You could also use a vehicle shuttle from the various put-ins. For the sake of brevity, I'll provide information about sections of the river beginning at the harbor in Old Town Bandon.

The Bandon waterfront is also home to Adventure Kayak, where a helpful staff can provide current information. They have a private launch available for use with permission.

## Bandon to Bullards Beach State Park

**Location:** Boat harbor in Old Town Bandon

**Directions:** From US 101 in Bandon, follow signs to Old Town and harbor.

*Paddlers make their way back into Bandon harbor after a trek up the Coquille River.*

**Facilities/Etc:** Improved restrooms, picnic tables, fishing docks at harborside; improved restrooms, day-use and camping at Bullards Beach State Park.

**Launch Sites:** Public docks or boat ramp.

**Length:** 2 miles one way

**Time:** 1+ hours

**Precautions:** Tree stumps, pilings and debris along the shoreline. Watch for fishing and recreational boats and for crabbing gear in the channel.

**Details:** Inquire at Adventure Kayak along the waterfront in Old Town Bandon for current paddling information. This is among the most scenic sections of the Coquille River, with plentiful birdlife and many interesting sights. From the harbor, cross the river and paddle north along the sandy riverbanks. As the river turns east, the shoreline becomes rocky as it approaches Bullards Beach State Park Boat Ramp. Sections along both sides of the river are part of the Bandon Marsh National Wildlife Refuge.

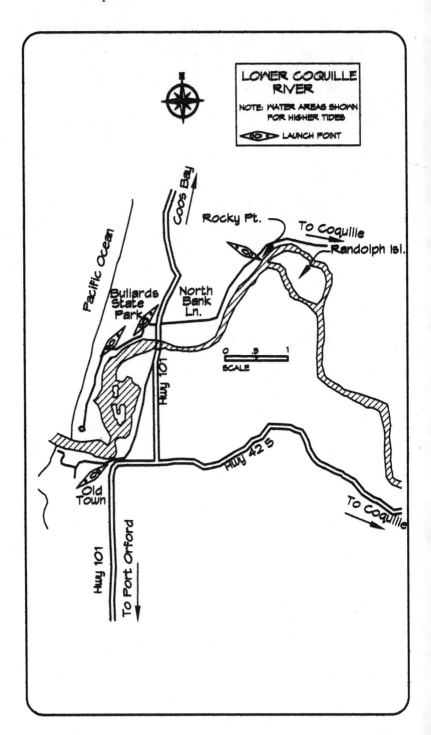

# Bullards Beach State Park to Rocky Point

**Location:** 2 miles north of Bandon.

**Directions:** From stoplight in Bandon at US 101 and Highway 42 S, head north on US 101 and in 1.7 miles cross the Coquille River Bridge. About 0.5 mile past the bridge turn west, following signs to Bullards Beach State Park. Follow road to boat ramp. Alternate launch site along sandy beach is 0.5 mile beyond.

**Facilities/Etc:** Vault toilets, day-use area, campground, yurts, equestrian campground, hiking and riding trails, lighthouse, ocean beaches.

**Launch Sites:** Public boat ramp, seasonal docks. *Alternate launch site:* Follow road to lighthouse another 0.5 mile beyond boat ramp to a sandy beach.

**Length:** 5 mile round trip.

**Time:** 1+ hours

**Details:** This paddle takes you through the heart of Bandon National Wildlife Refuge. You'll paddle beneath Coquille River Bridge, passing old fishing boats and remnants of Indian fish weirs. Upriver is Prosper, once a pioneer settlement with mills and fish plants. In later years many of the homes acquired blue metal roofs, and the site was considered for a marina. You'll pass Rocky Point County Park boat ramp, a potential stop. Turn around here and return downriver. You can extend this trip about 3.1 miles with a paddle around Randolph Island, just upriver from Rocky Point. The island forces the rivers into two channels. Take the north channel around the island, then return downriver in the south channel.

## Rocky Point and Randolph Island

**Location:** 1.1 miles upriver from the junction of the North Bank Rd. (near Bullards Beach State Park) and US 101.

**Directions:** From stoplight in Bandon at US 101 and Highway 42S, head north on US 101. Cross the Coquille River Bridge, and in 0.2 mile turn east on North Bank Ln., and follow it 1.1 miles to Rocky Point County Park.

**Facilities/Etc:** Vault toilets, picnic tables.

**Launch Site:** Boat ramp, dock, grassy embankment. Launch about 1 hour before high tide time at Bandon/ocean beaches.

**Length:** 3.1 miles total round trip, around island.

**Time:** 2 hours. High tide is approximately 30 minutes later than high tide at Bandon/ocean beaches. Paddle at near-high tide as you will be paddling both up and down river.

**Precautions:** Submerged or partially submerged logs and debris in river, especially during or after seasonal rains. Watch for old pilings. Fishing and recreational boats can create wake.

**Details:** The river splits into two channels as it goes around Randolph Island. Paddle up the north channel, passing the community of Randolph. Pilings are remnants of early-day docks for sawmills. Nowadays it's quiet paddling; you might even spot a harbor seal. Continue around the island and follow the south channel back downstream to Rocky Point.

## Rocky Point to Riverton

**Location/Directions/Facilities/Launch Site**: See previous tour.

**Length:** 9 miles one way.

**Time:** 3 hours

**Precautions:** Watch for floating limbs, branches and debris.

**Details:** This tour passes the site of the pioneer-era settlement of Parkersburg, and includes peaceful stretches where the shoreline roads are well away from the river.

# Riverton to Coquille

**Location:** 10 miles east of Bandon.

**Directions:** From US 101 in Bandon, take Highway 42 S, following signs to Coquille. In about 9.1 miles, turn north into parking area for Riverton Boat Ramp.

**Facilities/Etc:** Vault toilet, picnic tables.

**Launch Site:** Boat ramp, riverbank.

**Length:** 6.4 miles.

**Time:** 2+ hours depending on tide and current.

**Precautions:** Watch for debris in river.

**Details:** Peaceful river paddle. Among the sights are three sets of pilings that once supported an early-day coal bunkering facility. The coal came from mines in nearby hills. You'll pass the outlet of Beaver Slough, as well as a water outtake for the Roseburg Lumber Co. mill and Cunningham Creek, just before Sturdivant Park.

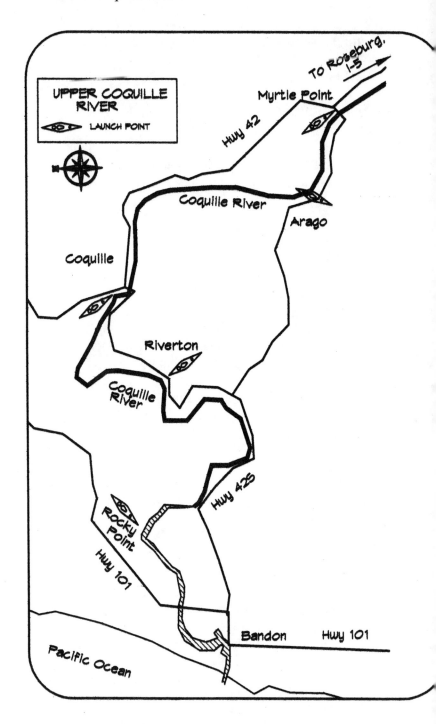

## Coquille to Arago

**Location:** About 20 miles east of Bandon, near city of Coquille.

**Directions:** From Bandon, follow Highway 42 S to Coquille. Cross bridge over Coquille River and turn west into Sturdivant Park, just before Highway 42 S junction with Highway 42.

**Facilities/Etc:** Vault toilets, picnic tables, seasonal camping. Park may be closed due to flooding in winter and spring.

**Launch Site:** Boat ramp, seasonal dock.

**Length:** 6.5 miles

**Time:** 3+ hours depending on current and tide. High tide at Sturdivant Park Boat Ramp is 3 hours later than at river's mouth.

**Precautions:** Watch for debris in river.

**Details:** Further meanders of the Coquille River. Sturdivant Park is the site of a historic spruce mill. Just upriver was the original waterfront of Coquille, but not a trace remains. Beyond that is a popular fishing spot called Dutch John Hole. You'll pass the city of Coquille's water outtake pumps, as well as Glen Aiken and Rink creeks. Johnson Log Pond and Dement County Park are along here, although it's hard to spot them from the water and there are few places to disembark. Three more creeks feed into the river before you arrive at Arago Boat Ramp.

## Arago to Myrtle Point

**Location:** About 25 miles east of Bandon.

**Directions:** From Bandon, take Highway 42 S, following signs to Coquille. In about 18 miles, at intersection with Highway 42, turn south, following signs to Roseburg. In about 7 miles, take Arago exit and follow signs to boat ramp.

**Facilities/Etc:** Vault toilets, picnic tables.

**Launch Site:** Boat ramp, seasonal dock.

**Length:** 4.2 miles

**Time:** 2+ hours depending on current and tide. High tide at Arago Boat Ramp is 3.45 hours later than at river's mouth, and 4 hours later at Myrtle Point.

**Precautions:** Watch for debris in water. Current can be strong in winter and spring — not recommended for travel during high water times.

**Details:** Under the right conditions this can be another enjoyable paddle up the Coquille River. You'll pass Grady Creek, as well as the confluence with the Coquille River's North Fork before arriving in Myrtle Point. Depending on river levels, it's possible to continue beyond Myrtle Point. (The river splits into its middle and south forks about 4.6 miles above Myrtle Point.)

# Beaver Slough

**Location:** 10 miles southeast of Coos Bay

**Directions:** From south end of Coos Bay, follow US 101 south 4.5 miles to "Y" intersection with Highway 42, and follow Highway 42 about 6.6 miles (11.1 miles total from Coos Bay) to North Bank Ln. Turn west on North Bank Ln. and cross bridge over railroad tracks, and another over Beaver Slough. Just past Beaver Slough Bridge, turn north

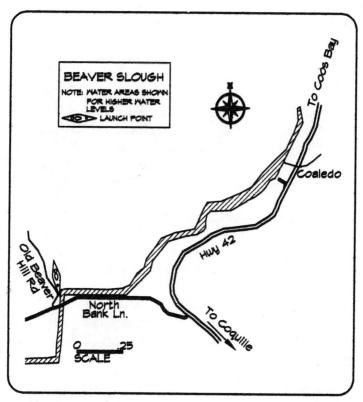

on Old Beaver Hill Rd. Bear right and park in an area just before a "Dead End Road" sign. A path leads down to the slough's edge. You might have to fight through blackberry vines.

**Facilities/Etc:** None.

**Launch Site:** Grassy embankment.

**Length:** 2.7 miles round trip, paddling to the ends in both directions.

**Time:** 2+ hours.

**Precautions:** Narrow winding channel usable mostly during winter and spring when water levels are higher.

Shorter boats will be easier to paddle in this area.

**Details:** This slough off the Coquille River was an important part of the region's early history, since it offered the easiest way to move people and goods between the Coquille Valley and the Coos Bay area. Small boats and canoes came up Beaver Slough from the Coquille River, then the goods were unloaded and carried over a rise of hills to Isthmus Slough, an arm of Coos Bay. The overland trek reminded settlers of crossing the Isthmus of Panama, hence the name Isthmus Slough.

As for the name Beaver Slough, it's easy to see how that was chosen, since evidence of beaver activity is still visible. In earlier times, it was a constant challenge to keep the narrow passage clear of dams. Beavers rebuilt their lodges nearly as quickly as they were knocked down.

You can paddle in either direction from the put-in, following the slough to its head, or back down nearly to its confluence with the Coquille River (an irrigation pipe blocks passage into the Coquille River.)

*Paddling up-channel*: Best in times of high water. You'll parallel railroad tracks and Highway 42, and pass under an old bridge. Farther along is Beaver Creek, which can be paddled for a short distance, passing under Highway 42. Watch out for submerged barbed wire fencing near the bridge. The main channel continues north to its terminus at an embankment.

*Paddling down-channel:* The slough passes under North Bank Ln. and flows into a straight channel between pasturelands. Continue paddling until you reach an irrigation pipe, which forces a turn-around.

## Johnson Log Pond

**Location:** 3 miles east of Coquille On Highway 42.

**Directions:** From Coquille, go south on Highway 42 2.7 miles and turn right on Johnson Mill Rd. Follow gravel road to pond.

*Alders form a frame around Johnson Pond.*

**Facilities/Etc:** Vault toilets, picnic tables, fishing dock.

**Launch Site:** Fishing dock.

**Length:** 1.6 miles (perimeter).

**Time:** 1 hour.

**Precautions:** Watch for many old pilings.

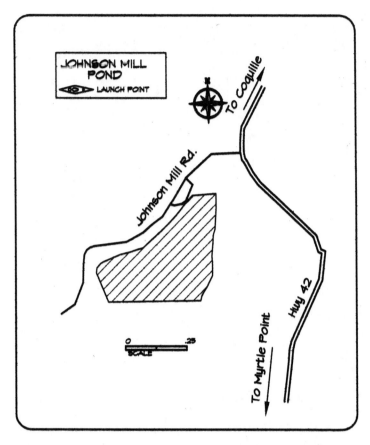

**Details:** This is a former storage pond for logs, now used for recreation and wildlife habitat. Birdlife abounds, and it's stocked with fish.

## Powers Pond

**Location:** Powers County Park, approximately 20 miles southwest of Myrtle Point.

**Directions:** From Highway 42 in Myrtle Point, continue east about 3 miles and take the Powers turnoff. Continue about 18 miles to Powers County Park, on the west end of town.

**Facilities/Etc:** Restrooms, picnic area, children's play

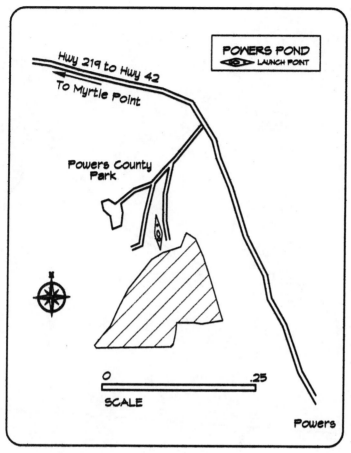

area, campground.

**Launch Site:** Boat ramp or grassy embankment.

**Length:** 1 mile.

**Time:** 1 hour.

**Precautions:** Watch for anglers.

**Details:** Another former log storage pond, this 40-acre lake offers easy paddling. It's stocked with trout and open for fishing year-round.

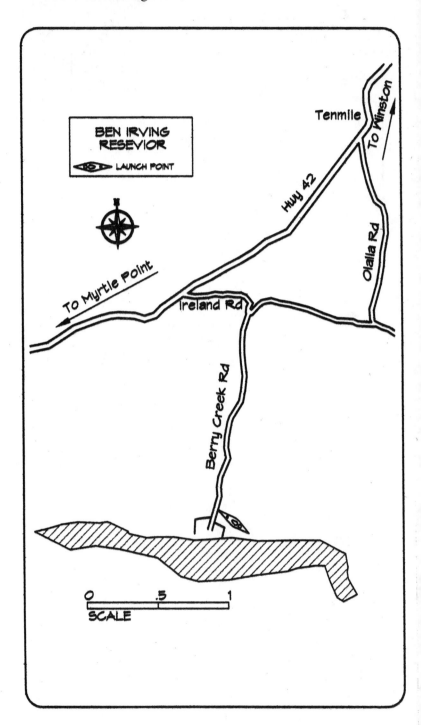

# Ben Irving Reservoir

**Location:** Near Tenmile, approximately 10 miles west of Winston off Highway 42.

**Directions:** Just west of Tenmile along Highway 42, turn left on Benedict Rd. near milepost 64, following the sign to Ben Irving Reservoir. (Eastbound travelers on Highway 42 can turn on Ireland Rd. near milepost 62, and follow signs to the reservoir.

**Facilities/Etc:** Vault toilets, picnic tables.

**Launch Site:** Boat ramp or sandy areas.

**Length:** 3.8+ miles

**Time:** 2 hours

**Precautions:** Some stumps and limbs in the water. Paddling to the left of the boat ramp will lead into an area of high-speed boats.

**Details:** I've included this paddle because if you're driving to or from the coast on Highway 42, it's a really nice place to take a "paddle break." From the boat ramp, the left end of the lake is used primarily by boaters. The lake's right end has boat restrictions, so this is the best section to paddle. Going that direction, 0.3 mile from the ramp, a 5 mile-per-hour restriction begins. At 0.8 mile from the ramp, a no-motor restriction begins and continues to the end of the lake. You could add another 3 miles to the tour by paddling the left section. Do so early in the morning or during the week in summertime. Little boat traffic will be found in the winter and early spring.

There's a freshwater wetland area with many birds and waterfowl sat the right end of the lake.

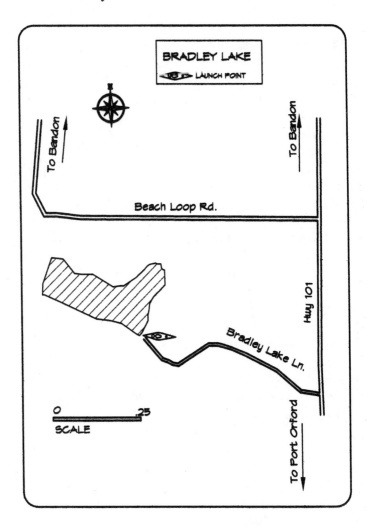

## Bradley Lake

**Location:** 4 miles south of Bandon.

**Directions:** From the stoplight in Bandon at US 101 and 11th Ave., go south on US 101 3.5 miles and turn west on Bradley Lake Ln., following it 0.6 mile to boat ramp.

**Facilities/Etc:** Vault toilets.

**Launch Site:** Boat ramp.

**Length:** 1 mile (perimeter).

**Time:** 30 minutes.

**Precautions:** Watch for overhanging limbs and floating debris.

**Details:** Small lake with wetlands. Much of the shoreline is private property. There are some sand dunes at the west end of the lake but are signed as private property.

# New River

**Location:** 5 - 15 miles south of Bandon.

**Directions:** There are three ways to access New River, one of which was still being developed as this book went to press.

  **Four Mile Lane:** (Under development) From the stoplight in Bandon at US 101 and 11th Ave., go south on US 101 about 7.3 miles and turn west on Lower Four Mile Ln. The paved road turns to gravel in about 2 miles, and swings north. At this writing the gravel road ends at a barricade about 1 mile beyond, at a county park. There's an adjacent parking area, and the sand road continues another 0.5 mile to the edge of New River, so a portage is necessary. This road will eventually be graveled to the edge of New River, providing year-round access to the north end of the river.

  **Storm Ranch**: From the stoplight in Bandon at US 101 and 11th Ave., go south on US 101 for 8.7 miles. Just beyond milepost 283, turn west on Croft Lake Ln., and follow it 1.6 miles. Take the right fork, following the sign to BLM New River Storm Ranch Area of Critical Environmental Concern. Continue to the Storm Ranch interpretive site. The road beyond Storm Ranch is closed March 15 to September 15 to protect the threatened western snowy

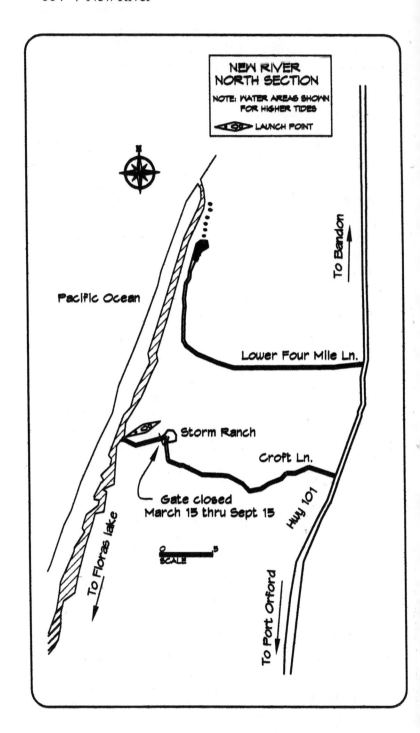

plover's nesting areas. *If the road is closed*: you can park here and portage your vessel the remaining 1 mile to the edge of New River. *If the road is open:* Continue past Storm Ranch and follow the road west, and at a "T" intersection in about 0.4 mile, turn north and follow the road to the parking area near the edge of New River. Launch from the river's edge.

**Floras Lake:** From the stoplight in Bandon at 11th Ave. and US 101, go south on US 101 15 miles to the community of Langlois. Continue south through Langlois and in 0.5 mile turn west on Floras Loop Rd., following signs to Floras Lake and Boice-Cope County Park. Continue west, then south, for 1 mile, then turn west on Floras Lake Rd., still following signs to Boice-Cope County Park. Continue about 1.6 miles to the park, situated beside Floras Lake. Launch from boat ramp or from the point south of boat ramp.

**Facilities/Etc:** Vault toilets and picnic tables are planned for Four Mile County Park. Storm Ranch has vault toilets, picnic tables at the interpretive center as well as at the river's edge put-in area. Floras Lake has improved restrooms, picnic tables, campground, bed and breakfast, and windsurfing board and kayak rentals. Day-use fee at Boice-Cope County Park.

**Launch sites:** See directions above.

**Length:** 9 miles (9.85 miles in winter) one way. Floras Lake to Storm Ranch — 6.7 miles. Storm Ranch to Four Mile Ln. access — 2.2 miles.

**Time:** 6+ hours

**Precautions:** Strong north winds must be considered, especially once you get close to the coastline at Floras Creek. Current will also be a factor depending upon the time of year. To avoid these winds, start early and watch for weather patterns. In winter and early spring, when and

*View from New River's north end.*

where the river enters the Pacific Ocean, watch for strong current and consider beaching your vessel for a rest stop and/or turning back a bit before the mouth. Paddling may also be difficult in shallow parts of the river. When the river is connected to the ocean, there will be strong tidal influences. These combined with heavy outflow of water and strong winds from the south may result in some challenging situations!

**Details:** Formed just over 100 years ago when a storm carved a new channel for Floras Creek, this unusual north-flowing river was supposedly named when a local rancher took a look and exclaimed, "It's a new river!" Access is limited since most of the adjoining land is private property. New River's main public access, at the BLM Storm Ranch

site, has a road closure to protect snowy plovers from
March 15 – Sept 15, necessitating a portage. The Four Mile
Ln. site is still being developed and also requires a portage.
The river actually begins as Floras Lake's overflow, so you
can start a trip at the lake and follow the river 9 or 10 miles
north, depending on the time of year and the river's water
level. Best paddling is during spring and early summer
months. In summer, the river at its northern end narrows
and narrows and finally fizzles out into a flat expanse of
beach near the Four Mile Ln. access site.  Winter and early
spring bring heavy rainfall, along with high surf and tides,
and under these conditions New River pushes north another
approximately 0.85 mile and carves an outlet to the ocean.
That vast expanse of beach becomes a floodplain during
high tide.

Such conditions also result in breaches of the dunes in
other places along New River, especially near Floras
Creek.

From a Floras Lake starting point, the channel is narrow
(about 20 feet wide), with the west side sheltered by
beachgrass-covered sand dunes. To the east are
pasturelands.

At 0.9 mile from Floras Lake is the Floras Creek conver-
gence with New River. The channel becomes much wider,
and depending on river levels, there's much more current.
(Also depending on river levels, you can paddle up Floras
Creek for a considerable distance, but again, plan on strong
current.)

At this point, the river turns west for about 0.4 mile, and
nears the Pacific Ocean and sandy beaches. The river
becomes quite exposed to north winds. Here also is where
the ocean often breaches the sand dunes during winter
storms.

Continue north for about 0.5 mile (distance from beginning = 1.8 miles) where the river narrows again and is
separated from the ocean by low dunes, which offer some
protection from the wind.

Strong north winds build up waves, some of which will

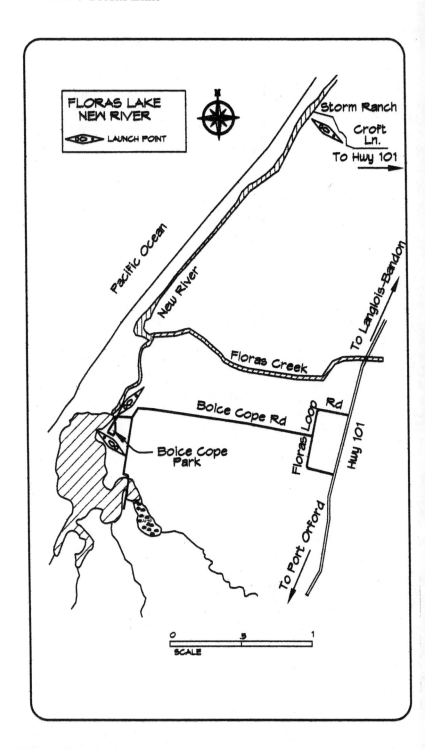

break in the middle of the river. Stick to the west bank, close to reeds and grass.

As noted, you can continue for 9 miles to the summertime terminus of New River, or approximately 9.85 miles to its wintertime seaward confluence, or turn around whenever you wish. Paddling on the return with a summer north wind at your back can offer some fun, surfing the wind-formed waves. You can also stop and explore the beach to the west, considered one of the most remote in Oregon.

## Floras Lake

**Location:** 3 miles southwest of Langlois.

**Directions:** From US 101 in Langlois, continue south on US 101 about 0.5 mile and turn west on Floras Loop Rd., following signs to Boice-Cope County Park. Continue west, then south, for 1 mile, then turn west on Floras Lake Rd., following signs to Boice-Cope. Continue 1.6 miles to the park and Floras Lake. At the south end of the county park is access to the windsurfing resort.

**Facilities/Etc:** Improved restrooms, campground, pay showers, bed and breakfast, windsurfing and kayak rentals. Day-use fee.

**Launch Site:** Boat ramp or point of land south of boat ramp.

**Length:** 5.2 miles (perimeter).

**Time:** 2+ hours

**Precautions:** North wind can be intense in summer. Plan paddles for morning. Watch for old pilings where the sandy bottoms meet the treeline.

**Details:** Floras Lake nestles just a few sand dunes away

from the Pacific Ocean, and is famous for its strong summer winds; a windsurfer's paradise! Yet it can he a delightful place to paddle on summer mornings or in the late fall and winter. Much of the lake bottom is sand, making it an ideal place for beginners and for paddlers wanting to practice advanced techniques.

From the boat ramp/county park area, paddle across the lake to the ocean side and follow the shoreline south. There are intriguing inlets, and river otters can often be found near the south end. Depending on the lake level, you can paddle into wetlands teeming with birds.

## Sixes River

**Location:** 6 miles north of Port Orford.

**Directions:** From Port Orford, follow US 101 north about 6 miles and turn east on Sixes River Rd., and follow it about 5 miles to put-in at BLM Edson Creek Campground. To reach take-out near Hughes House, turn west off US 101 about 5 miles north of Port Orford on road to Cape Blanco State Park and go 4 miles to day-use area below Hughes House. (See regional map page 11.)

**Facilities/Etc:** Vault toilets at Edson Campground. Portable toilet at Hughes House day-use area. Camping at BLM Edson and Sixes River campgrounds and Cape Blanco State Park. Cape Blanco Lighthouse is open for tours.

**Launch Site:** Boat ramp at Edson Campground. Boat ramp/grassy embankment at Hughes House.

**Length:** About 5 miles.

**Time:** 2 hours.

**Precautions:** Paddle only when river levels permit in winter and spring.

**Details:** One of two Wild and Scenic Rivers in the Port Orford area, the Sixes offers a beautiful, easy paddle – as long as there's enough water in it. As noted above, paddle only in winter and spring, and follow the river as it flows into a wide coastal plain near the sea. The take-out is in a day-use area beneath some magnificent cypress trees, along a stretch of river just below historic Hughes House, a restored pioneer-era ranch house that's open for tours and is part of Cape Blanco State Park.

# Elk River

**Location:** About 4 miles north of Port Orford.

**Directions:** From Port Orford, follow US 101 north about 4 miles and turn east on Elk River Rd., following it 10 miles to the Elk River Fish Hatchery. (See map page 11.)

**Facilities/Etc:** Portable toilet at fish hatchery. USFS Sunshine Bar and Butler Creek campgrounds located farther up Elk River Rd., as are a number of unimproved campsites. Cape Blanco State Park has a campground.

**Launch Site:** Gravel bank just west (downriver) of fish hatchery. Take out site is about 1 mile up Elk River Rd. adjacent to parking area for driftboaters.

**Length:** About 10 miles.

**Time:** 2-3 hours.

**Precautions:** Paddle only when river levels permit in winter and spring.

**Details:** Like the nearby Sixes, this is a Wild and Scenic River that offers a serene, beautiful paddle when there's enough water. This is a favorite of local paddlers, although it 's a rainy season paddle only. Conditions change so frequently that some paddlers say it's "always a different river." Put in just downriver from fish hatchery. The take-out is tricky to see from the river; watch for strips of surveyor's tape tied to trees at the site. *Watch carefully for it, because paddling back up the Elk is extremely difficult.*

## Garrison Lake

**Location:** Port Orford.

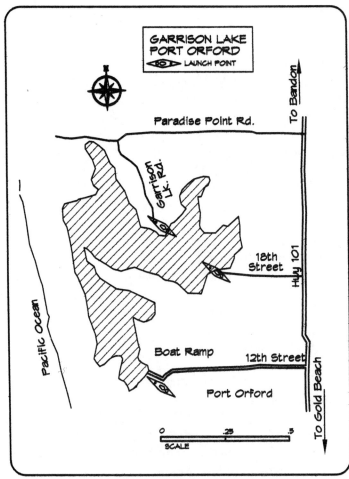

**Directions:** From central Port Orford, go north on US 101 to 12th St. and turn west, following signs to the boat ramp.
*Pinehurst Fishing Dock put-in:* Proceed as above, and turn west off US 101 on 18th St. and follow it to lake's edge near seasonal fishing dock.
*Paradise Pt. put-in:* From central Port Orford, go north on US 101 1.3 miles and turn west on Paradise Pt. Rd. In 0.4 mile turn south on Garrison Lake Rd. and follow it to gravel boat ramp at lake's edge.

**Facilities/Etc:** Vault toilets, picnic tables at state boat ramp. None at other sites.

**Launch Sites:** See directions above.

**Length:** 4.4 miles (perimeter).

**Time:** 2+ hours.

**Precautions:** Seasonal flooding may prevent access to main boat ramp. Paddle well away from Port Orford's municipal water intake pipe. Watch for tree limbs and stumps. Be alert for recreational boaters.

**Details:** Fairly shallow lake with several arms to explore. It's separated from the ocean by a sandspit, with many custom homes along the shoreline. Follow the lake in a counter-clockwise direction. Birdlife abounds; egrets and herons work the water's edge. Along the lake's western shore by the ocean are many places to pull up on the sand and explore the beach.

# Rogue River

The Rogue River starts its 215-mile journey to the Pacific Ocean far up in the Cascade Range, near Crater Lake. It's popular for fishing, swimming, boating, rafting and paddling for nearly its entire length. So popular, in fact, that permits are required to float, boat and paddle along certain stretches. There are Class V rapids in some places, but as it nears the sea, the Rogue settles down to offer current-assisted paddling through some of Oregon's most spectacular scenery. At this writing, no permits are required to paddle below Foster Bar.

Out and back excursions in the river's estuary near Gold Beach can be fun, challenging and rewarding. Tidal influence extends about 4 miles upriver. While the Rogue's current can be strong, it's actually a series of pools and riffles

In summer, a persistent north wind in the afternoon and dazzling sunshine (when the fog burns off) can be important factors to consider.

Most trips from upriver sites require a vehicle shuttle. There are a handful of easy put-ins/take-outs at US Forest Service campgrounds and other locations.

Whether you start within sight of the ocean or 30 miles upriver, the Rogue River offers paddlers a memorable experience.

**Location:**  Gold Beach

**Directions:**  To access Port of Gold Beach boat ramps, follow signs from US 101 to harbor area. To access upriver sites, head north on US 101 and turn east just before the bridge on Rogue River Rd.

**Facilities/Etc:**  Vault toilets at USFS Foster Bar, Quosatana and Lobster Creek campgrounds, and at Hunt-

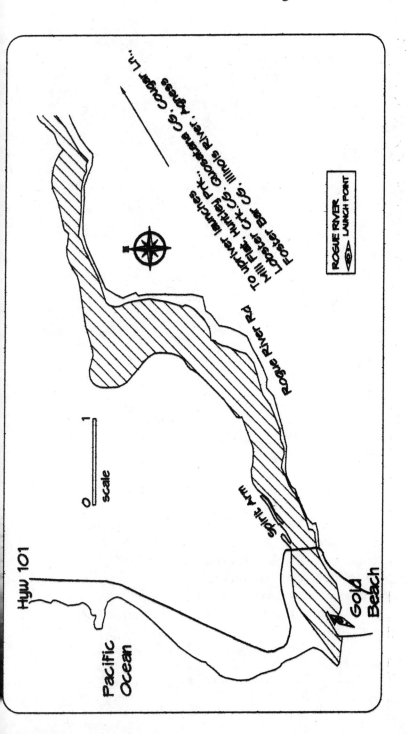

*With Lobster Creek Bridge in the background, kayak paddler Leanne O'Neil enjoys a Rogue River trip.*

ley Park. Improved restrooms at Cougar Lane and Port of Gold Beach. Camping at USFS campgrounds listed above. Camping and RV park at Cougar Lane. RV parks and full services in Gold Beach.

**Launch Sites:** Boat ramps and docks at Port of Gold Beach.
Upriver sites (All mileages from US 101/Rogue River Rd. intersection):
*Riverview Restaurant*: 1.6 miles. Boat ramp.
*Mill Flat:* 5 miles. Gravel bar.
*Huntley Park*: 8 miles. Gravel bar.
*USFS Lobster Creek Campground:* 10.7 miles. Boat ramp, gravel bar.
*USFS Quosatana Campground:* 14 miles. Boat ramp, gravel bar.
*Cougar Lane Resort:* 28 miles. Gravel bar.

*USFS Foster Bar Campground:* 33.5 miles. Gravel bar.
*Oak Flat (llinois River):* 30 miles. Gravel bar.
**Length:** Varying depending on trip.

**Time:** 1 hour to 2 days, depending on length of trip.

**Precautions:** Current can be strong, especially in winter and spring. Two-mile Rapids (2 miles downriver from Foster Bar) is a challenging, Class II+ rapids; use caution. Summer wind in afternoons can be strong near ocean, while sun reflection on water and summer heat can be intense; try to paddle in the morning.

**Details:** As noted above, you can put in and take out at a variety of locations. One of the most enjoyable paddles actually begins in the Illinois River, a tributary of the Rogue River, upstream from its confluence with the Rogue. Follow Rogue River Rd. about 27 miles and turn east on Oak Flat Rd., and go 3 miles to its dead-end at a gravel bar at river's edge. The Illinois is noted for its sparkling-clear water, and is underlain with serpentine rock that creates luminous green pools and sunken grottos. It takes about an hour to reach the Rogue River, and another 4 hours to get to Quosatana Campground (and longer to further downriver sites.)

Speaking of Quosatana Campground, this is an excellent place to launch an out and back trip up through a little visited and impeccable part of the Rogue River. You can paddle through miles of pools and riffles, practicing technique against the eddies and currents, or "walk" your vessel through sections you're unsure of. You're in total control of your time and distance, but a 2 mile trek upriver is an easy and fun way to start.

*Total distances and times from farthest upriver sites:*
Foster Bar to Gold Beach: 33.5 miles; 6 hours
Oak Flat (Illinois River) to Gold Beach: 35 miles; 6 hours.
*Incremental distances and times:*

Foster Bar to Agness/Cougar Lane Resort: 5.5 miles; 2 hours.
Cougar Lane Resort to Quosatana Campground: 14 miles; 5 hours.
Quosatana Campground to Lobster Creek Campground: 2.8 miles; 1 hour.
Lobster Creek to Huntley Park: 2.7 miles; 1 hour.
Huntley Park to Mill Flat: 3 miles; 1 hour.
Mill Flat to Port: 5 miles; 2+ hours.

*Rogue River Estuary and Spirit Arm:*  Put in at Port of Gold Beach boat ramps, Riverview Lodge boat ramp or Mill Flat. Tidal influence extends 4 miles upriver. Spirit Arm, so-named by local paddlers, was once the main branch of the Rogue, and provides about a half-mile of paddling in a beautiful setting rich with wildlife and waterfowl.

## Hunter Creek

**Location:**  South of Gold Beach

**Directions:**  From Gold Beach, follow US 101 south 2 miles and turn east on Hunter Creek Rd. Go 5 miles to steel bridge across Hunter Creek. *Take your boat out immediately after crossing under the US 101 bridge*, just before the ocean entrance at Kissing Rock. (See regional map page 11.)

**Facilities/Etc:**  None.

**Launch Site:**  Grassy/gravel embankment just downstream from large rocks in river.

**Length:**  5 miles

**Time:** 1-2 hours.

**Precautions:**  Paddle only when river levels permit in

winter and spring, and watch for tree limbs and other debris.

**Details:** This is another of the small rivers that locals call "rain responsive," since it can only be paddled when storm runoff brings up its level. But when it's right, it can be fine, fine and fun!

# Pistol River

**Location:** 11 miles south of Gold Beach on US 101; 17 miles north of Brookings.

**Directions**: From Gold Beach, follow US 101 south 11 miles and turn west at Pistol River State Park. (From Brookings, follow US 101 north 17 miles.) *Upriver launch site:* go south 0.2 mile from Pistol River State Park and turn east on Carpenterville Rd. Turn north at next intersection and follow road across bridge over Pistol River. Turn east on North Bank Pistol River Rd. In 1.2 miles turn right into parking area marked by an Oregon Dept. of Transportation sign, and another identifying this an "Access Watch" area. This site is used by anglers and driftboaters, so don't block the river access road.

**Facilities/Etc**: None.

**Launch Sites**: Sandy riverbank at Pistol River State Park. Depending on water levels, you might have a shorter walk from a parking area at the north end of the 101 bridge. Gravel bar at upriver site.

**Length:** Pistol River State Park upriver to ODOT site: 2.1 miles. Pistol River State Park downriver to Pacific Ocean (northern arm): 1+ miles. Southern arm: 1 mile.

**Precautions:** Paddle only when river levels permit. Low river levels expose rocky riverbed in places and impede access to southern arm and Pacific Ocean.

*Ocean breakers lie just beyond the sand dunes as a kayaker makes his way down Pistol River.*

**Details:** One of many small Coast Range streams that meander to the Pacific Ocean, Pistol River has a short stretch of fun paddling as it nears the sea. You can start at a state park near the ocean and paddle upriver and back, or drive upriver, launch and paddle down and back. The mouth of the river, where it meets the sea, varies depending on the season, and can be "bar bound" (sanded in) in late summer and fall.

In addition, a channel adjacent to Pistol River State Park extends south for about 1 mile, traveling through low sand

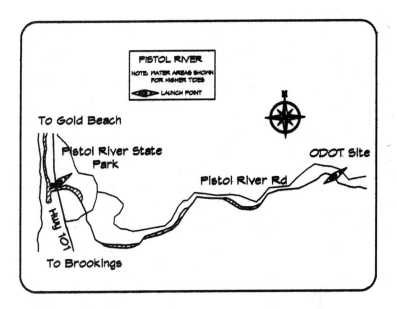

dunes and ending in a lagoon. Depending on water levels
and tides, the channel sometimes connects to the river.

## Chetco River

**Location:** Brookings.

**Directions:** From stoplight in central Brookings (US 101
and Center St.), follow US 101 south 0.5 mile. To access
river near its ocean confluence, turn west just before
Chetco River Bridge and follow signs to the harbor.

To access upriver sites, follow above directions and turn
east just before the bridge, on North Bank Rd. See notes in
"Launch Sites" for upriver mileages and details.

**Facilities/Etc:** Improved restrooms at Port of Brookings
Boat Ramp; vault and portable toilets, primitive and improved camping at upriver sites.

**Launch Sites:** Boat ramp, dock at Port of Brookings.
Gravel bars at upriver sites. Following mileages from

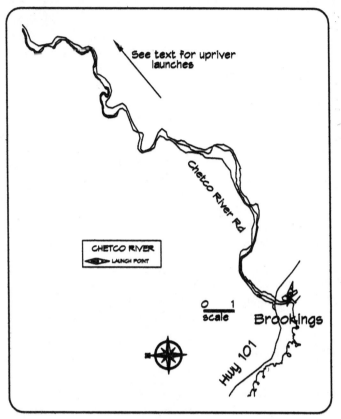

intersection of US 101/North Bank Rd.:

*Joe Hall Creek:* 1.5 miles. Gravel bar access.

*Gauging Station*: 2.5 miles. Gated road used by anglers leads to gravel bar.

*Social Security Bar:* 3.2 miles. Gravel access bar.

*Gravel Bar:* 4.3 miles. Near big intake structure. Gravel road to water's edge; gravel bar access.

*Willow Bar Public Access:* 6.7 miles. Gated gravel road to easy gravel bar access.

*Loeb State Park:* 7.4 miles. Boat ramp and gravel bar access.

*Forest Service Boundary:* 7.8 miles

*Bridge over Chetco River:* 8.7 miles

*Boater Registration Box:* 9.9 miles

*Miller Bar:* 10.2 miles: Access road twists 0.8 mile down to gravel bar along river. Primitive camping, portable toilet.
*Nook Bar:*11.4 miles. Primitive camping, improved toilet, gravel bar access.
*USFS Little Redwood picnic area:* 12.4 miles. Portable toilet, trail to river, gravel bar access.
*USFS Little Redwood Campground:* 12.6 miles. Seasonal campground.
*Redwood Bar:* 12.8 miles. Primitive camping, portable toilet, gravel bar access.
Pavement ends: 15 miles.
*Lower South Fork:* 15.3 miles. Primitive camping, portable toilets, gravel bar access.
*South Fork Bridge:* 15.5 miles. To access Chetco Gorge Trail and put-in, turn left at T intersection with FS 1917, following sign to Packer's Cabin. In about 0.5 mile, turn northwest on FS 200, following sign to Chetco Gorge Trail, 0.5 mile. This low-water hiker crossing (and site of former bridge) has a riverbank lined with large rocks, making launching difficult, but it's possible under the right conditions to wade in and launch from shallow gravel areas.

**Length:** Varying depending on trip. The road pretty much follows the river so mileages listed above roughly correspond with river miles.

**Time:** Varying depending on trip. Downriver trips have current to speed up the usual 3-mph paddle rate.

**Precautions:** Watch for the occasional submerged tree or half-sunken tree limb. Low water in summer and fall may require short portages. Don't block river access for driftboat anglers.

**Details:** You can put in or take out at access points for more than 15 miles up the Chetco River, and have a lot of fun paddling between them. Because of the current, longer trips require a vehicle (or bicycle) shuttle. Your reward is

*Soaring mountains, tall trees and beautiful, clear water add up to fine paddling on the Chetco River near Brookings.*

some of the most beautiful paddling described in this book. Small, smoothly-rounded rocks line the riverbottom, shore-lines and "gravel" bars, with many sandy interludes and lots of places to get out of your boat. There's a self-service permit registration station for all watercraft users but no fees are required at this writing.

# Winchuck River

**Location:**  5 miles south of Brookings, just north of Oregon-California border.

**Directions:**  From stoplight in central Brookings (US 101 and Center St.), follow US 101 south 5.1 miles. Just beyond Itzen Rd., turn west into the day-use area at Winchuck River.
To access upriver sites, turn east Winchuck River Rd. USFS Winchuck Campground is 9 miles.

**Facilities/Etc:**  Vault toilets at day-use area and Winchuck Campground. In addition to the campground, there are undeveloped campsites.

**Launch Sites:**  Sandy beach and grassy areas at day-use area; easy riverbank put-ins at upriver sites.

**Length:**  1-9 miles depending on amount of exploration and river levels.

**Time:**  1+ hours.

**Precautions:**  Water levels may be too low for paddling from upriver sites. Watch for logs and limbs in water. Use caution where river meets the ocean: be alert for sneaker waves, high surf and waterborne logs.

**Details:**  Because of low water levels in summer and fall, this small river is best explored by starting near its confluence with the Pacific Ocean, at the day-use area noted above. Paddle upriver as far as water levels and your

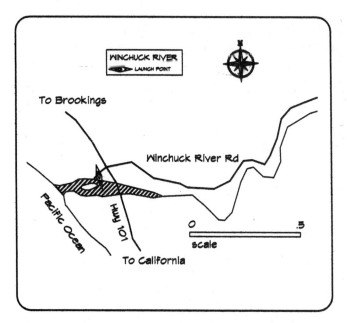

energy permit. Consider launching about 1 hour before high tide and use the incoming tide on the trip up, and the outgoing for the return. The river goes through beautiful, peaceful farmlands and past many custom homes. Local paddlers note that the Winchuck's level does not vary as much, nor is its current as fast, as its neighbors the Smith and Chetco rivers.

*Ron Wardman*

## ABOUT THE AUTHOR

Retired from a 30-year teaching career at Myrtle Point High School, Ron Wardman is an architectural draftsman who enjoys paddling, bicycling, windsurfing, motorcycling and exploring the Pacific Northwest with his wife, Toni.

A native of Colorado, he attended the University of North Colorado, and received a masters degree from Western Oregon State College. He's built several sailboats, as well as a redwood canoe, and joins in many of the sailboat races and events at the Coos Bay Yacht Club on Ten Mile Lakes in Lakeside. He and Toni live in Myrtle Point and enjoy frequent visits with their children and grandchildren.

## NOTE FROM THE AUTHOR

Special thanks to my editor and publisher, Tom Baake. I met him at a local trails meeting and mentioned my tour book in progress. He offered to help me complete it. My vision was a rather simple guidebook but he helped me make it a much better and more usable book for paddlers. I'd also like to thank fellow paddlers Dick Vigue, Reed Lockhart and Terry Dill, who joined me on many of these the tours.

## NOTE FROM THE PUBLISHER

Your help is very much appreciated! If you have comments or suggestions for future editions, please let us know. Updated information will be posted on our web site, *www.scod.com/guidebooks.*

   E-mail publisher: *westways@harborside.com*
   E-mail author:   *cwardman@gte.net.*

## ABOUT THE PHOTOS & ARTWORK

Thanks to Ned Reed of *Charts, Maps and Graphics* in Bandon for the use of his original drawings, and for information about Coquille River and Bandon, technical support and design consultation.

Thanks to Jim Coffee of Gold Beach for information about Rogue River, Hunter Creek and Elk and Sixes rivers.

Thanks to Frank Babcock for bringing out his handmade white cedar canoe for some of the photos.

Thanks also to Bob Carr of *Adventure Kayak* in Bandon for help with photos, information, and ongoing support.

Thank you Reed Lockhart for paddling insight and editorial review.

Thanks to Linda Eger for creative and editorial contributions, design consultation, and logistical support.

Photo on page 73 by Iain D. P. Karroll. Photo page 126 by Jim Coffee. All others and book design by Tom Baake.

Cover photo is of McCullough Bridge from North Spit launch point described on page 65. Frontispiece photo is of Lone Rock, in Haynes Inlet, described on page 77.

Thanks to all the folks who let us use photos of them!

## TRAVEL TIPS, MILEAGES AND DISTANCES

US 101 is "main street" of the Oregon coast. It hugs the shoreline in some places and ranges more than 10 miles inland in others, but it connects just about every town along the coast.

Unless you're coming down US 101 from Washington, or up from California, you'll have to traverse the Coast Range on one of several state highways to get here. Travel on all these routes is considerably slower than interstate speed. This is especially true in summer, when the roads are busy. Summer is also road construction season, adding further delays. Allow plenty of time for travel.

A brief rundown of east-west highways: Highway 199: Grants Pass to Crescent City: 92 miles. Twisting and turning through the Coast Range, it dips into California to meet US 101 just north of Crescent City.

Highway 42: Roseburg to Coos Bay: 85 miles. (Roseburg to Bandon via Highways 42 and 42S: 82 miles.) Fastest east-west route to the south coast, with passing lanes and smoothed-out curves.

Highway 38: I-5 to Reedsport: 70 miles. Scenic drive with many stretches following Umpqua River. Slightly less busy.

Highway 126: Eugene to Florence: 80 miles. Popular route with lots of summer traffic and a few challenging curves on the western descent of the Coast Range.

Generally speaking, in summer months it's advisable to choose the east-west highway that takes you as close as possible to your destination, so as to minimize travel time on US 101. When you get stuck in the inevitable long caravan of cars and trucks and motor homes and trailers, you'll see the wisdom of this tip.

US 101 mileages: Crescent City, Calif. to Brookings: 27 miles.
Brookings to Gold Beach: 26 miles.
Gold Beach to Port Orford: 25 miles.
Port Orford to Bandon: 25 miles.
Bandon to Coos Bay: 24 miles.
Coos Bay to Reedsport: 28 miles.
Reedsport to Florence: 21 miles.

## HELPFUL PHONE NUMBERS

US Coast Guard Emergency Line Only (541) 756-4141
US Coast Guard Charleston/Coos Bay (non-emergency) (541) 888-3266
US Coast Guard Umpqua River/Winchester Bay (non-emergency) 541-271-2137
US Coast Guard Chetco River/Brookings (non-emergency) 541-469-2242
Marine weather: (541) 888-3102   Aviation weather: (541) 756-0135
Oregon Dunes National Recreation Area, Reedsport (541) 271-3611 Florence 902-8526
South Slough National Estuarine Research Reserve, Coos Bay (541) 888-5588
Bureau of Land Management, Coos Bay (541) 756-0100
Oregon International Port of Coos Bay, Charleston Marina (541) 888-2548
Coos County Parks Department, Coquille (541) 396-3121 ext. 354
Oregon State Parks, Southwestern Division, Coos Bay (541) 888-8867
US Forest Service Gold Beach District (541) 247-2133
US Forest Service Chetco District, Brookings (541) 469-2196
Florence Chamber of Commerce 1(800) 524-4864
City of Dunes City (Slitcoos Lake and River) (541) 997-3338
Reedsport Chamber of Commerce (541) 271-3495
Lakeside Chamber of Commerce (541) 759-3981
Bay Area Chamber of Commerce, Coos Bay 1(800) 824-8426
Bandon Visitors Center (541) 347-3480   Port of Bandon (541) 347-3206
Port Orford Chamber of Commerce (541) 332-8055
Gold Beach Chamber of Commerce 1(800) 525-2334  Port (541) 247-6269

Brookings Chamber of Commerce 1(800) 535-9469   Port (541) 469-2218
Central Coast Watersports, Florence (541) 997-1812
Lakeside Marina, Lakeside (541) 759-3312
Sunset Sports, North Bend (541) 756-3483
Surplus Center, Coos Bay (541) 267-6711
Discovery Boat Rentals, Coos Bay (541) 888-9389
Adventure Kayak, Bandon (541) 347-3480
Rogue Outdoor Store, Gold Beach  (541) 247-7142
Escape Hatch Sports, Brookings (541) 469-2914
Get continuous weather info on VHF: 162.4 mHz

Websites:  www.coostrails.com
            www.oregonsbayarea.com
            www.or.blm.gov/coosbay
            www.scod.com/guidebooks

*Let's paddle!*

Paddlers' notes

Location:
Directions:
Facilities/Etc:
Launch Site:
Length:
Time:
Precautions:
Details:

## PADDLERS' NOTES

Location:

Directions:

Facilities/Etc:

Launch Site:

Length:

Time:

Precautions:

Details:

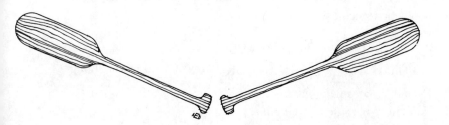

*Have fun exploring all the wonders of Oregon's spectacular south coast!*

# Out Our Back Door

### DRIVING TOURS AND DAY-HIKES
### IN OREGON'S COOS REGION

Head any direction along Oregon's south coast and discover a recreational wonderland -- from the vast Oregon Dunes, to lakes, rivers and waterfalls, to miles of unspoiled, lovely beaches.

From seaside to mountaintop, let this guidebook lead you to the region's world-famous scenery, and to some of its overlooked treasures.

Coos Bay outdoor writer Tom Baake explores the region's popular scenic spots and visits the "back road" places, with an emphasis on easy day-hikes and driving "loop" tours. Among destinations are the spectacular seaside gardens at Shore Acres State Park, the twin cascades at Golden and Silver Falls State Park, and South Slough, the nation's first protected estuary.

You'll pass through parts of Coos, Curry, Josephine, Douglas and Lane counties on back-country byways, with plenty of places to stop for a picnic and fun.

Wander through old-growth forest, some containing specimens of the world's largest trees, and see unusual geology, inspiring waterfalls, soaring ridges, and intriguing slices of life, both two and four-legged. Wildflowers, wild rhododendrons and azaleas line the way on many of the roads, while autumn colors are a delight.

There's information on camping, biking, boating, paddling, fishing, even a chapter on "what to do on a rainy day." Most of all, it's a book about picnics -- so let's go!

## WESTWAYS PRESS

440 Third Ct.        Coos Bay, OR  97420        (541) 269-5833

E-mail:    *westways@harborside.com*
Website:  *www.scod.com/guidebooks*

Available at book stores and gift shops
Order directly ($10) from publisher and get free shipping!